ELVIS

WORLD

ALSO BY JANE AND MICHAEL STERN

TO JAN LEVI AND KEN SOFER

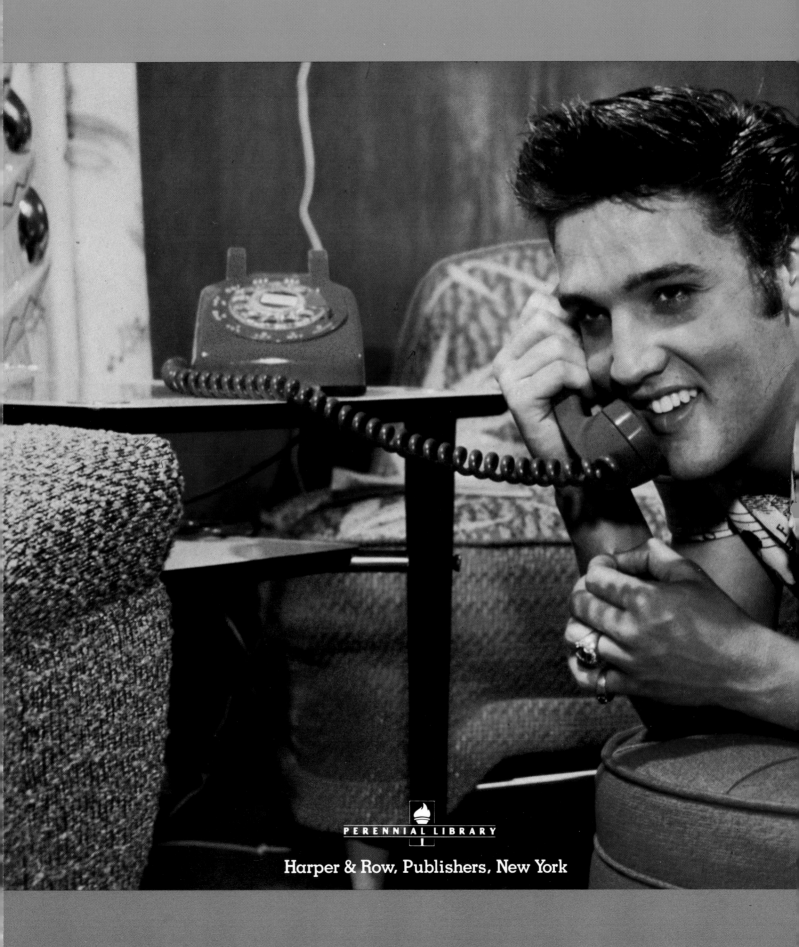

PERENNIAL LIBRARY

Harper & Row, Publishers, New York

ELVIS WORLD

Jane & Michael Stern

LIBRARY OF CONGRESS CATALOG CARD NUMBER 89-46120

ISBN 0-06-097290-4

90 91 92 93 94 KP 10 9 8 7 6 5 4 3 2 1

Contents

Introduction

Welcome to Elvis World. This book is intended as your guide.

Elvis World is not one place. It is the universe defined by all he stands for: music, of course, and movies, but also the cascade of material things he consumed, the fans he enraptured and stuffed shirts he outraged. Ten years after his death, Elvis World is thriving, built around the provocative symbol Elvis continues to be.

Filled with pink Cadillacs, blue suede shoes, galaxies of gold records, cheeseburgers galore, and roller coaster rides till dawn, this is a world where dreams came true for a poor boy born in a two-room shack in Tupelo, Mississippi.

At the heart of Elvis World are the true believers, fans who consider the forty-two years, seven months, and eight days he spent on earth close to sacred. They are the ones from whom we got the title of this book. Elvis World is always on their minds and in their daily conversation. They talk about Elvis World anniversaries, marking important dates of his life; or they explain their code of ethics by saying, "We in Elvis World prefer to focus on the good that Elvis did."

Elvis World has a real geography: the grade-school auditorium in Tupelo where he first stood up to sing; Hollywood, where he lived while making movies; Bad Nauheim, Germany, where he was stationed in the Army; and, most important—Graceland, his mansion on a hill. Pilgrims come to Memphis to visit Supercycle, where he bought his Harley-Davidsons; the pizzeria that displays his karate belt and a lock of his hair; the now-dilapidated housing project where he lived as a teenager and was teased by neighboring kids who called him "Velvet Lips" Presley. Shrines include any place he shopped, ate, bought cars or guns or diamond rings.

Strange as it seems, Elvis the artist—deemed by the Smithsonian Institution to be the most important voice in the history of American music—is of limited importance in Elvis World. Observe almost any gathering of devoted Elvisites. His music is played, but attention will likely focus more on the singer than on his songs. The songs, like the movies, are only manifestations of Elvis; listening is a way of being close to him. Leave it to critics to analyze his impact on modern music or the piano glissandos in "Money Honey." As good as it was, music is not the essence of Elvis World. Elvis is.

It isn't only the hard-core fans who relish Elvis beyond his music. Ask the man on the street to name ten things about Elvis, and he could probably reel off: pompadour, Cadillacs, blue suede shoes, wiggling hips, sneering lip, Priscilla, Graceland, "The Ed Sullivan Show," was rich, got fat. Ask for ten songs and you might get five. Ask for ten movies and you'll get a shrug.

Elvis has always been known for his looks, his image, the details of his insolent style. When he was young, America went nuts not only over his music but over his sideburns, his wiggle, and his bodacious clothes. When he got fat, his weight was reviewed with as much zeal as his performances. Since he died, best-sellers have been written trading on outrageous revelations about his eating habits, his drug use, and his grumpy moods. Elvis has always been an issue way beyond his art.

Gossip mongers relish Elvis. But tabloid slander is not the true road into Elvis World. To get mired in the dirt is to miss the exaltation. Whatever his health problems, they were scrupulously kept private when he was alive. And now that he is dead, they are nothing more than a banal footnote to a career that was extraordinary in every other way. To make more of them than that is a Pyrrhic victory of cynicism over art.

To understand the Elvis mystique, you must know details: the pink-and-black pants he bought on Beale Street when he was eighteen; the roots of his hair (blond) and its progress from well-oiled ducktail to blow-dried, mutton-chopped, blue-black helmet. You have to know about the souvenir lamps he bought for his mother, Gladys, and the proper way to grill his favorite peanut butter and banana sandwich.

Elvis World is founded on physical truths, not philosophy. It is a world of bits and scraps, things and places from his life: his fur-covered bathroom scale, on display at the Elvis Hall of Fame in Gatlinburg; the hardware store in Tupelo to which busloads of admirers from around the world journey so they can see the exact spot where he bought his first guitar.

We drew our picture straight from Elvis World: fan club bulletins, scholarly analyses, and bubble-gum trading cards; the records and the movies; and the indelible images that so many of us carry of exactly where and when we were affected by the Elvis phenomenon. We spent time with fans and fan clubs, impersonators, collectors, and ordinary people whose lives brushed his.

Minute details of Elvis World are doted over by fans, but you don't have to be one of them to feel a part of its history. Many of us bore witness to such unforgettable moments as Elvis's induction in the Army, Priscilla's towering wedding coiffure in 1967, and the tabloid exploitation of his death at age forty-two. It was a great, glittering saga which Bruce Springsteen has called "horrible, and at the same time, fantastic."

Elvis is a landmark in almost everyone's life, going back to distant memories of watching him above the waist on Ed Sullivan or hearing "Hound Dog" for the first time. His image continues to mesmerize: witness the appearance of two hundred Elvis impersonators at Liberty Weekend in 1986.

There was a time when he was merely the most popular entertainer in history. He is more than that now. He is a symbol of America as recognizable as the flag. Show his picture to a taxi driver in Thailand or a housewife in Tasmania or a ten-year-old child in Bangor, Maine, and they will all recognize him. While working on this book, we never once met anyone who asked, "Elvis who?"

You don't have to be a fan. You don't even have to like rock and roll. Just hop in the pink Sedan de Ville and come with us. Even if you don't want to live there, Elvis World is an amazing place to visit.

ELVIS WORLD

The Shock of Elvis

It's 1956. Ginny and Elizabeth are thirteen years old. They are making plans to faint.

"If he looks at me, I am going to faint."

"If he points in my direction, I'll faint."

"What if he sees me faint and comes off the stage to help revive me?"

"Then I am going to die on the spot."

Unconsciousness is the natural effect of Elvis Presley on the delicate nervous systems of pubescent girls.

Like South Seas maidens preparing for some awesome tribal ritual, Ginny and Elizabeth are readying themselves to succumb at an Elvis Presley concert.

Their ceremonial garments have been selected weeks in advance. Elizabeth, a hep kitten, sports an angora sweater with a chiffon scarf knotted at the neck and a grey felt circle skirt with Elvis's face glittering in rhinestones on the front. On her wrist jingles a bracelet with a charm for each of her favorites of his hit records. His name is embroidered twenty-five times on her canvas hat. Each of her sneakers bears his likeness.

Ginny, who plans on impressing Elvis with her sophistication, wears a draped pink crepe dress with a matching hat selected from the Montgomery Ward catalogue because it is described as "gay and pert." On her feet are Cuban heels dyed to match. On her hands, of course, are white gloves.

The girls have shaved the fuzz from their legs, rubbed Mum under their arms, anointed themselves with official Elvis Presley Enterprises Teddy Bear Eau de Parfum, and rouged their lips Love Me Tender Pink.

They carry no crook or votive candle; their scarabaeus is a Brownie Hawkeye, loaded with a fresh roll of Verichrome Pan, flashgun ready.

Joining a thousand others like themselves, they sweep toward the door of the theater ready to fall prostrate at the feet of their idol: Elvis the Pelvis, the Atomic-Powered Singer.

Ginny's pink crepe hangs close, wilting fast with nervous perspiration. At the sight of the poster outside showing him head back, legs spread, guitar cocked, and mouth open, she screams. And like a pack of hunting dogs picking up the fox's scent, all the girls around her scream, too. Every time a Cadillac drives past, they scream. When the policemen herd them through the barricades, they scream. When the ushers open the door, they scream. By the time they have reached their seats they are hoarse and wet—and the house lights haven't even dimmed.

It is midsummer, and, as in all the concert halls Elvis Presley plays, there is no air conditioning. Smells of perfume and laundry starch mingle with the panting breath and sweat of the fans, who are as agitated as wild animals before an earthquake. Some are starting to pass out already.

The curtains part. The girls simultaneously shriek and hold their ears. Then a mass groan rumbles through the auditorium as the emcee announces the first of a procession of stinkeroo acts: lame-brain comics, second-rate magicians, jugglers, yodelers, trick dogs.

Mississippi, September 1957. "Hound Dog." Elvis in rapture with RCA's mascot, Nipper.

An hour later, the tension has risen to ominous proportions, expressed by the incessant chant of "WE WANT ELVIS." Finally, when the last rabbit has been pulled from the last hat and the Jordanaires have sung their last spiritual, Elvis Presley hits the boards.

He stands in the spotlight and begins to rock: "I got a woman way 'cross town, she's good to me. . . . " The gust of noise expelled by the crowd blows dust off the heavy red velvet curtain. The humid lust of thousands of teenage girls rolls toward the proscenium and is volleyed back by each thrust of his body.

Inside his billowy suit strange things are going on. Knees are flapping; everything is twitching so bad it looks like a skinny man having an attack of claustrophobia inside a tent.

He is up on his toes, on the sides of his feet, carried across the stage by legs with a life of their own. He is down on the boards with a death grip on the microphone, he is up pounding the flat back of his guitar with his belly.

His face is as startling as his body. In repose, the profile is Michelangelo's *David:* classical Grecian nose flattened and straight as a rule, venting hot breath above pouty lips. But it is seldom in repose. The mouth twitches and grimaces, flickering from a sneer to a boyish smile. The eyelids, low and lush, tinted by nature a pale iridescent brown, and by mascara a sooty black, hang heavy over pale blue eyes that shimmy in and out of focus.

Like buttercream frosting on a cake, his hair is his crowning glory. Depending on the month and the performance, it ranges from light brown to black. What is constant is the great gob of pomade, a glistening brilliantine of good-ol'-boy viscosity like Dixie Peach or Lover's Moon, raked into the locks so thick that you can count the furrows dug by the tines of the comb.

The tonsorial pyrotechnics are not just a hairdo, no mere wad of mane to keep the head warm and the hat cushioned. Hair is his trademark and his strength. It has a life of its own, more than the sum of the parts that

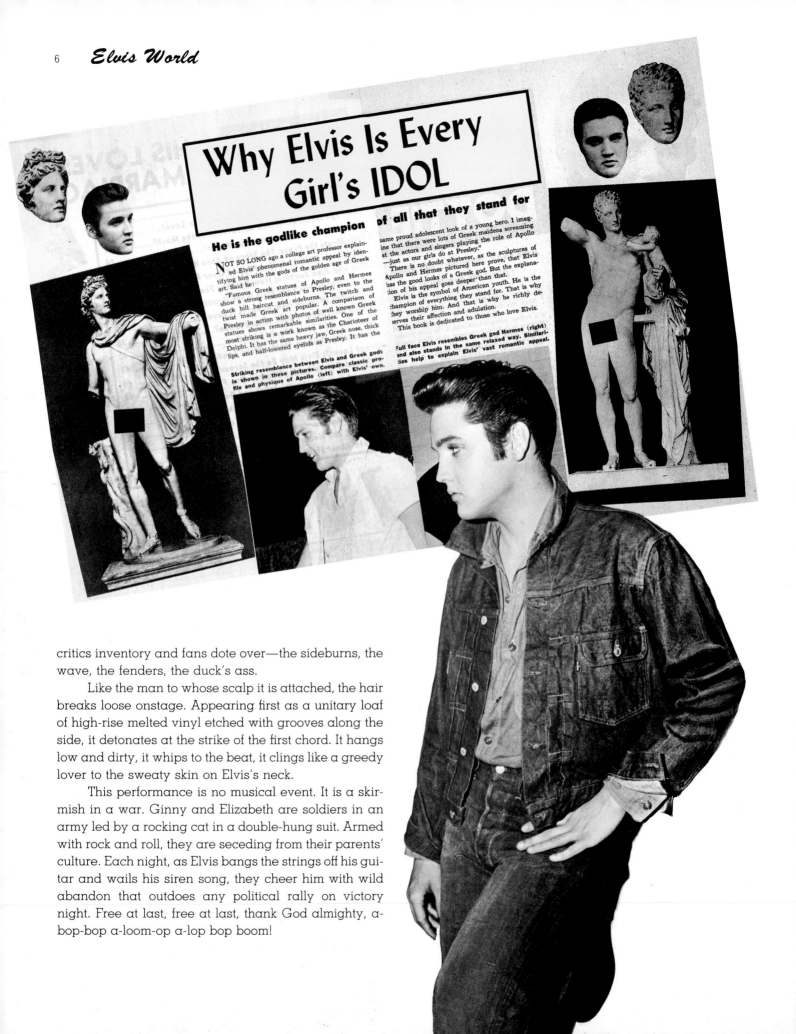

Why Elvis Is Every Girl's IDOL

He is the godlike champion of all that they stand for

NOT SO LONG ago a college art professor explained Elvis' phenomenal romantic appeal by identifying him with the gods of the golden age of Greek art. Said he:

"Famous Greek statues of Apollo and Hermes show a strong resemblance to Presley, even to the duck bill haircut and sideburns. The twitch and twist made Greek art popular. A comparison of Presley in action with photos of well known Greek statues shows remarkable similarities. One of the most striking is a work known as the Charioteer of Delphi. It has the same heavy jaw, Greek nose, thick lips, and half-lowered eyelids as Presley. It has the

same proud adolescent look of a young hero. I imagine that there were lots of Greek maidens screaming at the actors and singers playing the role of Apollo —just as our girls do at Presley."

There is no doubt whatever, as the sculptures of Apollo and Hermes pictured here prove, that Elvis has the good looks of a Greek god. But the explanation of his appeal goes deeper than that.

Elvis is the symbol of American youth. He is the champion of everything they stand for. That is why they worship him. And that is why he richly deserves their affection and adulation.

This book is dedicated to those who love Elvis.

Striking resemblance between Elvis and Greek gods is shown in these pictures. Compare classic profile and physique of Apollo (left) with Elvis' own.

Full face Elvis resembles Greek god Hermes (right) and also stands in the same relaxed way. Similarities help to explain Elvis' vast romantic appeal.

critics inventory and fans dote over—the sideburns, the wave, the fenders, the duck's ass.

Like the man to whose scalp it is attached, the hair breaks loose onstage. Appearing first as a unitary loaf of high-rise melted vinyl etched with grooves along the side, it detonates at the strike of the first chord. It hangs low and dirty, it whips to the beat, it clings like a greedy lover to the sweaty skin on Elvis's neck.

This performance is no musical event. It is a skirmish in a war. Ginny and Elizabeth are soldiers in an army led by a rocking cat in a double-hung suit. Armed with rock and roll, they are seceding from their parents' culture. Each night, as Elvis bangs the strings off his guitar and wails his siren song, they cheer him with wild abandon that outdoes any political rally on victory night. Free at last, free at last, thank God almighty, a-bop-bop a-loom-op a-lop bop boom!

Elvis was making America flip.

Jeanelle Alexander, president of the Shreveport-Bossier (Louisiana) Elvis Presley Fan Club, defined "flipping" as experiencing "in an extreme form and simultaneously the emotions of love, hate, anger, hero worship, and anxiety."

"My feeling during the show," wrote Chloe Lietzke in *Elvis Now—Ours Forever*, a collection of reminiscences by fans, "was a total unconsciousness of myself. . . . I was compelled to keep my concentration on him every minute! On a deep level, I was totally 'there,' but on a conscious level, I was not there."

Arlene Cogan, author of *Elvis This One's for You*, remembers being part of a mob of ten thousand fans doing battle against one hundred policemen, forty firemen, and two hundred ushers. "Two guys hanging from the balcony railing dropped down into the mob, apparently to get closer to Elvis. One girl kicked an usher in the stomach and they carried him out with the others who apparently had fainted."

Florida, August 1956. Fans suspect Elvis is on board.

As Elvis moved through the land like chain lightning, one community after another registered the shock. He came, he sang, they flipped, and he moved on. "For days following," Chloe Lietzke recalled, "I was still in a dream world. I remember wanting time to stand still, because, as the days went by, I was farther away from Elvis."

His effect was like no other entertainer's before him. The bobby-soxers' shrieks for Sinatra now seemed so tame. Bing Crosby's bababooms, even Johnny Ray's most emotional convulsions, were spring showers compared to the Elvis storm. The only thing comparable to the Elvis phenomenon was the landings of aliens in flying-saucer movies. The population looked on in awe and horror. Teens fell under his spell. They grew sideburns and pledged undying fealty to their new master.

Elvis *was* an alien in Eisenhower America. While middle-class Joes with squared-off brush cuts were barbecuing weenies on the patio or mowing the lawn in plaid bermudas, he was buying pink Cadillacs and pegged pants and lace shirts with a peekaboo effect.

He appeared onstage in jackets that hung down to his knees. He wore a diamond pinky ring in the shape of a horseshoe. Unlike Dapper Dan crooners never seen without sharp threads in a handsome pose, he was photographed by the fan magazines in a state of deshabille, lounging half-naked on a motel bed like an odalisque in a seraglio.

The same year Elvis burst upon the scene, Allen Ludden authored *Plain Talk for Men Under 21!*, cautioning his readers that "originality is fine, but don't be an odd ball."

There was no odder ball than Elvis.

The words that poured forth when he sang were as weird as his looks: "shake, rattle, and roll" . . . "flip, flop, and fly" . . . "tutti frutti, au rutti." . . . This was the nonsense argot of the underclasses. Nice people were supposed to listen to singers who shaped their vowels and measured their phrasing. But Elvis's young fans gobbled up the saturnalia, ingesting naughty lyrics even if they didn't fully comprehend them. The hit parade of sappy love songs was obliterated by thumping, nonverbal sensuality.

And the *way* he sang! No critics paid attention to the sweet songs. What they heard was an impatient voice off the streets—arrogant, angry, looking for trouble. He gnawed on lyrics and spat them out ("Jailhouse Rock"); he barked ("Ready Teddy"); he moaned ("Hard Headed Woman"); he shook with passion ("Heartbreak Hotel"); his callow voice sailed high and broke from ecstasy ("Mystery Train").

When Elvis's first record was played on the air, disc jockey Dewey Phillips called him into the studio to tell the audience that he had attended Humes High School—reassurance to listeners in the segregated Memphis of 1954 that Elvis was indeed a white man.

Nobody had ever heard a white man (or a black man) sing like Elvis. White southern singers were supposed to be hillbillies. When Elvis—billed early in his career as "The Hillbilly Cat"—performed at the Grand Ole Opry, they told him to go back to truck driving.

As a hillbilly artist, he was a fraud. He didn't wear boots and fringe, he didn't wail mountain-pure laments about lost love, he couldn't yodel very well or play the ukelele. In fact, by Opry standards, he couldn't even play the guitar properly. He was notorious for breaking the strings out of unbridled enthusiasm each time he took the stage. To Nashville, Elvis and his Memphis eccentricities might as well have come from the far side of the moon.

To the rest of the country, his southernness was equally perplexing. He wasn't a cute funny southerner in overalls and straw hat like Tennessee Ernie Ford on "I Love Lucy." He wasn't from the mint-julep antebellum South, or the South of clog-dancing mountain men and colorful old quiltmakers. Tupelo, where he was born, is scarcely fifty miles from William Faulkner's home. It was the weird, mysterious, sexual South, the South of poor whites and poorer blacks who scratched their living from the dry earth; of chain gangs and Holy Roller services raising the devil and smiting him down again.

Who exactly was this pale, voluptuous, truly Faulknerian creature who slouched and sneered and spat rock and roll across the nation? In December 1956, *Cosmopolitan* posed the question that America had been asking for a year: "What Is an Elvis Presley?" It didn't know what to answer, except to hope that he would vanish as fast as he had arrived.

As much as anything Elvis sang, or his wiggles, or his looks, it was the bat-out-of-hell suddenness of the phenomenon that staggered the country. Eighteen months before he was acclaimed as the King of Rock and Roll, the biggest sensation in music history hadn't even cut a record.

On July 5, 1954, as Memphis suffocated beneath heat and humidity so intense it fogged the windows of stores and houses, a nineteen-year-old truck driver named Elvis Presley went into the Sun Records studio with Scotty Moore and Bill Black in hopes of coming up with a hit sound. In earlier sessions, Elvis had tried every Dean Martin ballad he knew, none impressing studio owner Sam Phillips.

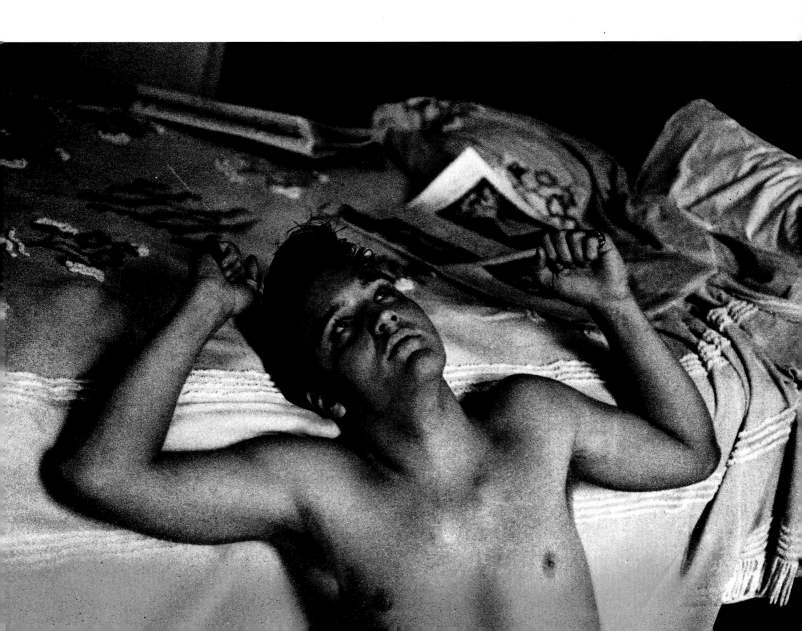

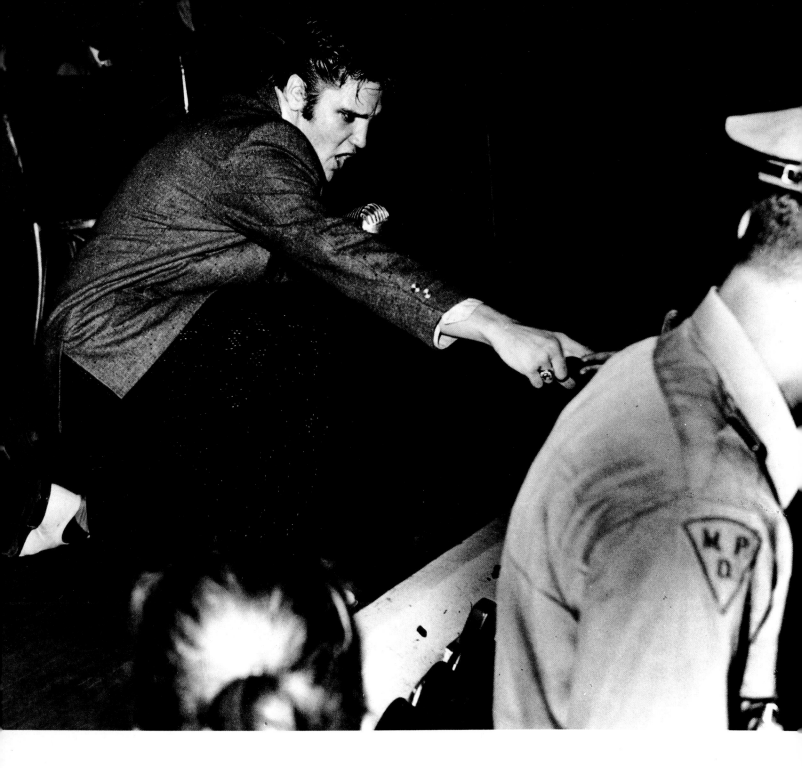

The trio recorded foot-dragging standards such as "Harbor Lights" and "I Love You Because."

Then, to relieve tension during a break, Elvis hollered out a superfast falsetto version of "That's All Right," a rhythm and blues song that Arthur "Big Boy" Crudup had recorded in 1946. Sam Phillips ran from the engineering booth into the studio, thrilled by what he was hearing. They recorded "That's All Right" nine times before coming up with a take they liked.

A demo was delivered to Memphis deejay Dewey Phillips (no relation to Sam) of WHBQ, who played it at 9:30 p.m., Saturday, July 10, on his "Red Hot and Blue" show. The station was deluged with calls. Dewey played the record thirteen times in a row. On Monday, Elvis, Scotty, and Bill formed a group—soon to be known as the Blue Moon Boys. A week later, Sun record number 209, "That's All Right" backed by "Blue Moon of Kentucky," was in the stores. By the end of the month, it was number 3 on the Memphis country and western charts.

"The odd thing about it," said Sun's Marian Keisker in a July 28, 1954, article in the Memphis *Press-Scimitar,* "is that both sides seem to be equally popular on pop, folk, and race record programs. This boy has something that seems to appeal to everybody."

That summer, Elvis performed in Memphis at the Bon Air Club and at Sleepy-Eyed John's Eagle's Nest and was added as an extra attraction at a July 30 show in Memphis's outdoor bandshell in Overton Park. The headliner was Slim Whitman. A newspaper advertisement listed Elvis third on the bill—as Ellis Presley. A

month later, he was paid ten dollars to play at the opening of Katz's Drug Store, performing from the back of a flatbed truck.

In November, he began appearing on the "Louisiana Hayride" radio show every Saturday night. For the next year he toured the South and Southwest, driving Cadillacs and Continentals to ten-and twenty-dollar bookings in roadhouses and school gyms. As the weeks passed, he was greeted by enthusiasm, then pandemonium, then riots. At one concert in a Mississippi high school, he was attacked onstage by girls hungry for a

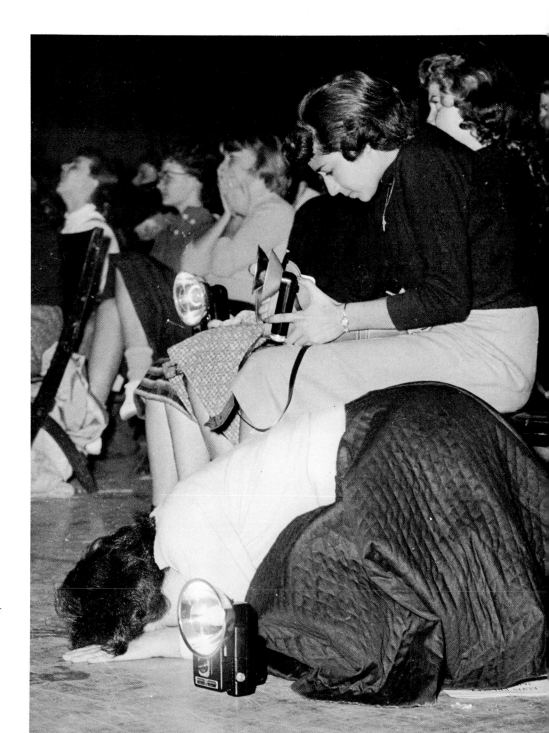

The first music Elvis heard was in church. Like an evangelist, he had the ability to make each person in the audience feel singled out and touched by his power.

When asked to explain why Elvis made her flip, one teenage girl told Mae Boren Axton (co-author of "Heartbreak Hotel"), "He's just one big hunk of forbidden fruit."

Fan Magazines

As the Elvis craze spread fast by radio and word of mouth, it was dutifully reported by newspapers and analyzed by major national magazines. But no one had a more riotous time than the fan magazines. What could be juicier? Elvis was a scandalous dream boat, nasty but nice, with a face that cameras adored.

Only fan magazines had the obsessive sensibility to document the minutiae of hero worship. Whereas *Harper's* studiously observed "The Man in the Blue Suede Shoes," calling Elvis "a *tabula rasa* on which the American populace could keep drawing its portrait, real and imaginary," *Modern Screen* offered pages of analysis about "What Really Bugs Elvis" (runny eggs) and "What Really Sends Elvis" (the color blue). It concluded

HOW PRESLEY INSPIRES OBSCENITY!

The Great
PRESLEY SCANDAL:
The "inspiration" his mob gets from Elvis erupts in catcalls dripping lewd vulgarities

BY MIKE HORTON

A Girl Confesses!

He's had me rockin' 'n rollin ever since

..."My Night with ELVIS PRESLEY!"

"We'd just said hello when 'The Pelvis' started kissing my fingertips...Then he kept right on going—and I was "gone!"

TURN THE PAGE

its enucleation of the real Elvis by divulging his secret password used with cousin Gene: "Goolytwash." No detail was too small to be important, no fact too trivial.

Movie Teen Illustrated revealed "What's Eating in Elvisville," listing lemon meringue pie, cherry angel-food cake, pork chops, hamburgers, spaghetti, and milk-chocolate peanut-butter cups as his favorite foods. It inventoried the beverages in his refrigerator: Pepsi, pineapple juice, Hawaiian Punch, and sarsaparilla. It described his favorite toys, including "those spooky boxes where you flip a switch and a little hand comes out of the box, flips the switch off, then disappears."

"Every fan is interested in what he wears, and when," *Movie Teen* noted, cataloguing "white slacks and bare back" in the morning, Bahama shirts tied calypso-style for horseback riding, leather and Levi's for motorcycle riding ("WOWEE!"), boxer shorts for sun bathing, lavender pants and pink jacket for nights out on the town. "You could wrap him in a sheet like Gandhi," the sartorial registry concludes, "and any girl would be drawn to Elvis Presley like a stray needle to a powerful magnet."

"Girls!" shrieked *Confidential*. "Beware of Elvis Presley's Doll Point Pen," alerting its readers to what it described as the latest fad in fandom: getting his autograph on one's bosoms, "Elvis on the Righty, Presley on the Lefty."

FIRST IT WAS ROCK 'N ROLL, NOW IT'S SKIN AND SCROLL...

Girls! Beware Of Elvis Presley's Doll-Point Pen

● **Leave it to Elvis the Pelvis to start new fads. You ought to see where he's signing autographs these days!**

Beware, girls. Elvis will sign his name at the drop of a shoulder strap!

Girls wrote letters to the *Elvis Yearbook* describing their Elvis dreams ("I was a plum in a pudding, and he stuck in his thumb"). They sent maps that gave Elvis directions to their houses. They reveled in "I remember" stories of times they actually touched him (or any of his garments), which was worth a hundred points on the Presley Patrol chart, compared to ten points for each clipping in the scrapbook.

The avid readership of fan magazines made them fertile ground for Elvis merchandising. Elvisiana of the 1950s was almost as big a phenomenon as the man himself. (It is said that along with Jesus and Mickey Mouse, Elvis's image has been reproduced more than that of any other character.) By the end of 1956, Elvis Presley Enterprises had sold $22 million worth of souvenirs; a majority of them dangled before eager teenage hearts and wallets in the fan magazines.

Alongside ads for freckle remover, fifty-nine-cent miniature palm trees ("Enjoy a touch of summer all year round"), and Chihuahuas that fit in teacups, the back pages of the teenzines were a cornucopia of Elvis rings, charms, dog tags, record cases, toy guitars, board games, black jeans, and blue suede shoes. There were glue-on sideburns, Tutti Frutti red lipstick, and Love Me Tender perfume. And there were hundreds of pictures of Elvis, little blurry snapshots for pasting into precious scrapbooks. They showed Elvis singing, standing, eating, yawning, and sleeping.

But wait—there was more! You could even win a date with Elvis! "Guys and Gals, here it is, the once-in-a-lifetime opportunity. For you gals a chance to date the boy wonder; for the guys, an opportunity to get a few tips on Elvis's magic."

Eighty thousand hopefuls entered the *Hit Parader* sweepstakes, explaining in a hundred words or less "Why I Want to Meet Elvis." The winner—her hundred-word entry lost in time—was Andrea June Stevens of Atlanta. With her mom as chaperone, Andrea was whisked to his side for a big night on the town. Decked out in a boat-neck sheath dress, she was treated to sandwiches in a coffee shop, a backstage visit, and a piano-side sing-along. The marvelous event was recorded in detail for all 79,999 of the losers to swoon over.

Fabian

Paul Anka

Ricky Nelson

Pat Boone

Edd "Kookie" Byrnes

Because he was the reigning King of Rock and Roll, the fan magazines pitted him against a barrage of pretenders to the throne. Among those offered up in battle by *TV Radio Mirror* were Paul Anka ("The Canadian Whirlwind"), Frankie Avalon ("Little But Lethal"), Edd "Kookie" Byrnes ("In Elvis's Hair"), Jimmy Clanton ("Hot Shot Southern Style"), Bobby Darin ("Has Knife, Will Travel"), Fabian ("Tiger on the Prowl"), Ricky Nelson ("Loaded with Blue Chips"), Lloyd Price ("Big with the Big Beat"), and Bobby Rydell ("120 Pounds of Talent").

Pat Boone was ranked number-one contender, although in late 1956, *TV Star Parade* announced that its reader poll to determine the undisputed champ showed Elvis the winner by a margin of 25,240 votes to Pat's paltry 10,153.

Nevertheless, fan magazines relished comparisons between the two, like Betty vs. Veronica or Liz Taylor vs. Debbie Reynolds. Mr. Naughty vs. Mr. Nice. They showed Elvis lounging bleary-eyed on a motel bed, or mashing his face down on his date's shoulder, while on the other side of the page, Pat Boone tucked his new daughter, Debby, into her crib. Elvis is seen raking in the dough, buying pink Cadillacs and fancy threads, making Hollywood movies. A picture of Pat is captioned, "TIME OUT: Movies must wait til he graduates from college in the east."

When Elvis entered the Army, the magazines had a field day predicting his demise. "The King of Rock and Roll Is Dead!" trumpeted *Movie Mirror* when Elvis was inducted. "Elvis Who?" asked another. And in a way, they were right. When Elvis returned in 1960, he was more popular than ever. But the primal hysteria was gone; and in a short time, the fan mags would have the Beatles to blither over.

piece of him. In the nick of time he was physically carried off the bandstand. His rescuers? His mother and father, who had come to hear their boy sing.

In August 1955, he signed a contract to be managed by Colonel Tom Parker. In November, RCA Victor bought his recording contract from Sun. The next month, CBS and NBC were bidding to see who got him first on national television.

Why all the ruckus? One thing about which everyone agreed: he was one strange cat. What people couldn't quite get into focus was the line between Elvis the primitive and Elvis the conscious artist.

Was he a con man playing out the fad for all it was worth? Was he as innocent about his devastating charm as he seemed? The slow talk, the easy manner, the lack of Ivy League aspirations: the boy was no egghead, that's for sure. (He was quoted by the New York *Daily News* as saying, "I'm strictly for Stevenson. I don't dig the intellectual bit, but I'm telling you, man, he knows the most.") On the other hand, there was no denying the shrewdness of his act.

From the very beginning, he was a prodigy of the slight gesture: a curled lip, a pointed finger, a twitch, a quick whomp of the knee. Like a healer who knows that pressure on each tiny nerve creates sensation in another part of the body, Elvis manipulated his audience with meticulous precision.

And yet he was doing things in public that looked as if they should be done only behind closed doors. His performances had the onanistic abandon of a horny teenage boy with his favorite dirty magazine. It was almost embarrassing to watch him! Did he know he was shaking and twitching? Or was he doing it all for you, because you liked to watch him do it?

Offstage, Elvis was just as enigmatic, walking a line between torrid and cool. Watch him on an early television interview on WRCA's "Hy Gardner Calling!" The screen is split; Elvis is asked stock questions: "How has your success affected you?" . . . questions any square would ask any hot young rocker. But rather than take the opportunity to show the world he was a regular guy by giving reassuring answers like "I'm so grateful for all that's happened," Elvis does the unthinkable: he answers honestly, candidly.

He says, "I'm all mixed up." He tells Gardner that he has trouble sleeping—just the way one would tell a friend who really cares. He droops on the couch and rubs his eyes and lets his mind wander, seemingly forgetting the television camera in front of him. By the time Gardner wraps the interview, Elvis is positively languid, melting into the cushions, closing his eyes restfully, futzing with his hair.

"Is it true you shot your mother?" Gardner asks. Elvis shakes his head and chuckles, "That one takes the cake." "What about the rumor that you get worked up before a performance by smoking marijuana?" At this question, Elvis distills the enigma of Elvisdom. He doesn't answer; he sinks lower, closes his eyes, looks to all the world as if he is in fact hooked on every drug known to man, and slurs out, "Idunno."

What concerned parent didn't suck in a startled breath at this evasiveness? What teen didn't thrill to his flirtation with danger? He didn't say yes; he didn't say no. Elvis the eternal tease scored again.

Was he aware of how odd he seemed to button-down taste? It is impossible to tell when you watch him on "Dance Party," a Memphis TV show hosted by Wink Martindale—the same firm-jawed Wink who today hosts game shows, who was then Memphis's Dick Clark. His interview takes place across a jukebox, over which Elvis—dressed in black and chewing a wad of gum—drapes himself like a study-hall poster demonstrating bad posture. He is as spacey as on "Hy Gardner." "I just came to say . . ." he tells Wink, "uh, I just want to say . . .What was it I came to say?" His eyes roll back and close, his voluptuous mouth curls up at the corner.

This was no Valentino or Rudy Vallee, over whom other generations had swooned. This was—in the words of *Life*—"a different kind of idol . . . deeply disturbing to civic leaders, clergymen, and some parents." Pat Boone was fine, the boy next door singing of a chaste kiss on a romantic shore. But Elvis broke every rule of polite behavior.

Take, for example, one of his favorite activities— combing his hair. *Manners for Millions*, one of the staunch etiquette books, declared public hair combing "A DISGUSTING ACT" and branded anyone who did it, "in such a way that dust, dandruff, or loose hair flies into the lap of the person near them, a most unrefined person." Elvis not only combed his hair in public, he looked lovingly into his hand mirror, he tweaked his crotch, he slouched and grunted and wiped his nose on his sleeve.

In the beginning. After his first record was released in the summer of 1954, Elvis toured the South and Southwest, first as one of the Blue Moon Boys (right), then with his own Elvis Presley Show. In February 1956, when photographer Robert Dye developed the picture at far right, he almost threw it away, worrying that his subject was sneering. Within months, that sneer would become part of the Elvis Presley legend.

Never mind his "yes, ma'am"s and "yes, sir"s; this boy was naughty.

If he was a Pied Piper whose call was irresistible to teens, where was he leading them? Parental nerves weren't calmed by their children's explanations of his charm. On May 14 , 1956, *Newsweek* quoted fans who said, "I like him because he looks so mean." "He's fascinating—like a snake." "I hear he peddles dope." "He's been in and out of jail, and he's gonna die of cancer in six months."

Nothing was more shocking about the Elvis phenomenon than the behavior of his teenage fans. What was America to make of its angora-clad daughters' frenzied reaction to his every twitch? It was as if he spoke a secret libidinal language with a message that sent them into spasms. "Teenagers are my life and my triumph," Elvis said in 1956. "I'd be nowhere without them."

Nice young girls, dressed in starched cottons and white gloves, were not supposed to heave and drool as if possessed by a grand mal seizure at the sight of some silly-named singing hillbilly. But Elvis turned them into hungry wolverines.

In New Orleans, six girls bound and gagged an elevator operator, captured Elvis, and held him prisoner between floors for an hour. In Hawaii, while he was walking from a hotel lobby to his car, fans attacked and took his shirt, ring, watch, and wallet.

In Jacksonville, he closed a set by joking, "Girls, I'll see you all backstage." They went berserk, fourteen thousand of them. They broke through police barricades, they cornered him in his dressing room, and they ripped off his clothes. The rags torn from his body were shredded into tiny scraps as the greedy girls fought for possession before Elvis's awestruck eyes. Rescued by the police, he was led to his car . . . but it had been discovered, too. They had broken in and stolen his collection of cigarette lighters, and the exterior was festooned with lipsticked love notes and phone numbers etched into the paint with fingernail files.

Every time Elvis pointed at a section of the crowd, it was as if electrodes sparked beneath their seats. They shrieked, moaned, fainted, and wet their pants. They crawled on hands and knees, pounding the floor. Reporters struggled to find words to describe them. In

Love Him Tender

The Presley Primer

A is for available; and we're all shook.

B is for Bible; his favorite book.

C is for Cadillacs in bright rainbow hues.

D is for Dottie who gave him the blues

E 's for East Tupelo: his birthplace, their boast.

F 's for his fans who dig him the most.

G is for "Graceland": to mansion from to hut.

H is for "Hound Dawg", who ain't nothin but.

I is for M.E. I'm his body and soul.

J : "Jailhouse rock", a great movie roll.

K 's for "King Creole." This is his latest.

L : "Love me Tender." Of songs, it's his greatest.

30

M is for Memphis, it's out of its rut.

N is for nothin', that a Hound Dawg ain't but.

O :Overton Park, his first taste of show biz.

P is for Parker. (the Colonel, that is.)

Q 's for your questions that put him on polls.

R is for Rhythm, and sweet Rock'N'Roll.

S is for sideburns; they're back on our man.

T is for teddy bears and thousands of fans.

U :Ultra or Utmost are words praising our hon.

V 's for pop Vernon, who's proud of his son.

W is for We; it's him we adore.

X is for the kisses we send him galore.

Y is for YOU, a prime favorite of his.

Z 's for the very livin, cryin End, —which he IS.

31

an Elvis fan tells all

By Evelyn Fraser, age 14, Long Beach, Calif.
(We have Movie Teen photographer Cosmo Gonzales to thank for the following "letter" from an Elvisite. Cos was standing on a Long Beach corner after El had invaded a malt shop there. Since Cos had the usual third hand (camera) dangling from one arm, Evelyn naturally assumed he'd been there to photograph El and might even be El's "court" photographer. So she cornered Cos and splattered him with Elvisworld questions: Does HE really give off yum-yum electricity, does HE really agree to sing to any girl who asks him in the right way, does HE have to exercise constantly to keep that build, does HE actually have an assistant who does nothing but keep his hair looking the insville way it does, etc., etc.? The only defense Cosmo could come up with was a question of his own. He asked Evelyn why SHE is so ape on El, to put it all on paper and deliver it to Movie Teen. He even gave her a dollar bill so she could buy a roll of film to photograph herself).

Close-up of an Elvis-Lovin' Fan

ANY ELVIS FAN naturally assumes everyone else is an Elvis fan. I mean, how did he get where he is unless everyone really likes him? So you can see I was surprised to have a friend ask me all kinds of questions about my being so crazy about Elvis. To me, it was as if someone asked me why I like to BREATHE! And then, wonder of wonders, I ran into this photographer for your magazine and HE asked the same question—why I'm so flipped for Elvis, and also asked me to put all my reasons on paper—so here they are as if everyone didn't know:

1. My number one reason would have to be his looks. Elvis is so handsome the sight of his picture gives me goose bumps. No one has those blue eyes with the merry-lovin' twinkle behind them. And I wish I had a slow-moving film of that smile. I'd like to watch the crinkles start at the corners of his mouth, the way his full, lower lip opens downward and spreads, showing his wonderful, even, sparkling white teeth. I could spend the rest of my days just watching that slow-motion picture of his smile from its first suggestion to its wide grin.

2. Elvis is so big and strong. Even his muscles have glamor and personality. You just KNOW he'd protect you and never let anything hurt you.

3. He's mature and manly. Period.

4. But with all his manliness, there's this sweet boyishness. You feel he'd be boss, but let you "baby" him just because he knows you'd enjoy it.

5. I've never known Elvis to sing a song he didn't believe in. If it's a ballad, he puts all his heart in it. If it's bluesy, he puts all his heart in it. No one has ever come even close to his style or his personal drive.

6. Elvis is wonderful in movies. I've seen them all — several times. He's so natural and you get all drawn in with the character he's portraying. But there's always the Elvis you love there, too, so anything he does is just right.

7. He's moody and restless, never dull. He likes to be on the go. It's special the way he likes to try new things and just plain have fun.

8. Elvis is good-natured, courteous and kind. And YOU know it!

9. Beneath his gentleness, you know there's rebellion, so you could never just take Elvis for granted or "file and forget." He keeps you interested at all times.

10. Like him? I love him for being devoted and loyal to his family and friends.

11. He believes in God and has strong faith.

12. Elvis has more energy than any two other boys I know. He likes sports and he likes to go boating. He's outgoing. He doesn't just attend an amusement park. He rents

"I'm sure I'm just one of millions"

"I sleep under an acre of Elvis pictures"

it for the day and likes to have his friends around him.

13. With all his success, he refuses to take himself too seriously. Elvis likes to let his hair down and have a good time.

14. Sometimes that moodiness I mention leaves him feeling strangely lonesome, troubled and worried. That's when I, like every girl in the world, would like to hold his head close and cuddle him understandingly.

15. You know you could confide in Elvis. You could tell him all your hopes and dreams and then he would tell you his.

16. Elvis loves little children and has contributed to many charities and organizations. He is helpful to the sick and handicapped children, a part of his personality you just have to admire.

17. He would be a real gas on a date. He has a really cute sense of humor and lovable good-heartedness.

18. No one has better taste in clothes. He has a flare for

brightness in clothes and I really go for his new continental-styled clothes.

19. It's the total Elvis that really gets you—everything he is.

And so to the second question I'm always asked, being such a complete nut for Elvis—how can you be so kook over someone you don't know?

I've never met Elvis, it's true, but you can't say I don't know him. I know so much about him, so many good things about him and I LONG so VERY MUCH to know more—everything I can about him. Every girl has a dream man and Elvis is mine. I know I have to share him with so many others, but Elvis fits everything I've ever longed for in THE man. I've read everything I could get my hands on that was about Elvis. I've studied every photograph, seen every movie over and over, listened to every record as many times as

possible and there's no question—Elvis is El with me.

I know there are some who say that a dream man in reality can be a disappointment, but I know in my heart that if I met him he would be everything I sense him to be . . . it could be no other way.

As to any special something about Elvis that makes me adore him, I can give no answer except to say that there isn't anything Elvis has ever done that I don't approve. I wish him well and know he will continue to be a success. If I'm just another fan, I'm glad to be called an Elvis fan. I think he has won a lot of support and I'm happy to be part of it.

I hope he reads this, because I'm sure I speak the sentiments of the thousands—hundreds of thousands—of girls who feel the same way.

Sincerely Elvis'
Evelyn

an Ottawa newspaper, they "sounded like fifty jet planes taking off at once." In the Los Angeles *Times*, they were "a volcano from which emitted an ominously growing cloud of smoke." In Atlanta, they were "an atomic explosion of juvenile emotion."

"The trouble with going to see Elvis Presley," the Detroit *Free Press* reported, "is that you are likely to get killed. The experience is the closest thing to getting bashed in the head with an atomic bomb."

"I don't know and I don't care," moaned one girl wearing an "Elvis for President" button when she was asked why Elvis affected her the way he did. "He's just wonderful. It's the way he does it. When he sings I get goose bumps all over. I just can't explain it."

Explaining Elvis became a national pastime —not among his fans (why explain it when you can feel it?) but among editorial writers, clergymen, psychiatrists, high-school principals, police chiefs, amateur professors of teenology, and culture-makers who found themselves overwhelmed by a baffling event over which they had no control.

Was Elvis merely a fad? A novelty, a musical anomaly of no more importance than hula hoops or Alvin and the Chipmunks? Jackie Gleason, the first man to put him on national television, declared, "I tell you flatly—he can't last."

The Fort Wayne (Indiana) *Sentinel* called him "a nice guy with a money making gimmick, riding it for all it's worth." When photographer Alfred Wertheimer was assigned to cover Elvis for RCA in early 1956, he shot almost everything in black and white—because even Elvis's record company figured his success wouldn't be long-lasting enough to warrant the added expense of color.

"I've heard that the lurchin urchin hasn't any kind of singing voice, and I was anxious to hear if there was anything to this rumor," wrote Hugh Thomson in an article for the Toronto *Star* entitled "Music(?) Review." Poor Mr. Thomson couldn't even get to first base. "After sixteen of his ballads, I still have no way of knowing. I just couldn't hear one note or one word he sang."

The music was irrelevant to what most of the exegetes found fascinating—Elvis's physical being. He was the "pouty lothario of the guitar" . . . "a sideburned bundle of the most enchanting, gyrating, and just plain drooling rock 'n' roll charmer ever to hit this world" . . .

Above: The most famous hairdo since Samson's was inspired by the swept-back sidewalls of southern truck drivers, Valentino's slicked-back conk, and the superhuman blue-black tint of Captain Marvel's coiff. Some girls even abandoned pincurls for Presleyesque forelocks and pseudo-sideburns.

Right: After the last note of "Hound Dog" at his 1957 concert in Tupelo, Mississippi, Elvis leaps off stage to escape 12,000 delirious hometown fans.

Elvis Presley Day

At the peak of his peak year, in late September 1956, Elvis went home—not to Memphis but to Tupelo, Mississippi, where he was born and where he lived until he was almost fourteen years old. The Presleys were poor when they left for Memphis, poor and from the wrong side of town.

What a triumphant homecoming it was! RCA estimated his first year's record sales were about to exceed ten million. Production was wrapping on his first feature film, *The Reno Brothers* (soon to be retitled *Love Me Tender*). His appearance on the Ed Sullivan show had just made ratings history.

Elvis came to Tupelo to perform at the Mississippi-Alabama Fair and Dairy Show. By dawn on the day of his appearance, the streets were thick with fans; the National Guard was called up to keep order. A homecoming parade was planned, but it had to go on without its hero: Elvis could not risk being caught in the open. When Mississippi governor J. P. Coleman arrived to present Tupelo's son with a scroll proclaiming September 26 "Elvis Presley Day," his car was mobbed by fans who thought he was Elvis.

It was hot; the thermometer hovered just below one hundred degrees when Elvis hit the outdoor stage for

the matinee show. He was dressed in a voluminous navy-blue velvet shirt made by his mother. His performance was pure Elvis, untamed by television censors. When he reached down to touch the outstretched hands of the audience, girls tore the rhinestone buttons from his shirtsleeve. Hundreds of fans wept hysterically. As he sang "Don't Be Cruel," one fourteen-year-old climbed onstage, accosted him, and held fast until she was pried away. Footlights were torn from their sockets. Reporters and photographers hid up onstage to protect themselves from the mob. The scene was so hysterical, Elvis stopped the show until the National Guard restored calm.

Before the evening performance, Elvis held court inside a canvas tent. Those who were there remember the heat as unbearable. Flanked by his parents and his new pal, movie star Nick Adams, Elvis posed for pictures. Car dealers, old girlfriends, school chums, teachers, friends, and relatives came for a look. Some hugged him, some cried with joy or jealousy; and they swapped stories about the way things used to be in 1945, when Elvis sang "Old Shep" during Children's Day at the fair and won second place: five dollars and free admission to all the rides, all day long.

America's 1950s leather boys. The Wild One of rock and roll stayed a Harley-Davidson man his entire life.

"a rube from rubeville" . . . "the missing link" . . . "the lad with the permanent sneer" . . . He looked "romantic" . . . "leering" . . . "sensual" . . . "hopeful" . . . "hungry" . . . "as if he has been affected by a serious case of stomach cramps."

The Minneapolis *Star* saw "a singing Valentino." In Atlanta he was "the singer with the profile of a Greek god and the motions of a Gilda Gray." When Jackie Gleason hired him to appear on his "Stage Show" television program, he described Elvis as "a Marlon Brando who can sing." He was also labeled "the wiggling James Dean," "the male Tempest Storm," "the baritone Marilyn Monroe," and "the singing Jayne Mansfield."

Like Jayne, early Elvis did seem like a comic exaggeration of sexuality. "A bulldozer in mating season" is what Hugh Thomson concluded, calling him "Mr. Overstatement." Whatever else he was, Elvis was indeed a product of his time—like tail fins, Cinerama, and the beehive hairdo. He flourished in a culture crazy for extremes.

But Elvis was something more than a symptom of mannerist America. All of the attempts to compare him with other entertainers fell flat, because he was an original. He had the same florid sexuality as Valentino, but he was no exotic sheik; he was a simple country boy. Musically, he contained the styles of rhythm and blues, country, gospel, and even a bit of hootchie-cootchie, but

he was not contained by any one of them. The raft of similes that floated his way in order to explain the significance of the Presley phenomenon was as meaningless as describing a king as a man who is like a high-school principal but wears a crown.

If Elvis had remained a stage performer, requiring payment of admission or the price of a record to be seen or heard, he might never have been so alarming. Elvis was dangerous because of television. All it took was the flip of a dial to bring him wiggling and shaking and shouting into the rumpus rooms of mid-century America. Parents could lock the doors and seal the windows to keep Elvis out, but there he'd be, winking from behind the glass screen.

Television had found its way into middle-class homes by 1956, but it was not yet taken for granted. The sets were massive major acquisitions with noble names to match. "The Aldrich," "The Westcott," and "The Chandler Deluxe" were three of RCA's new models for 1956—handsome consoles built to occupy a place of honor among household furniture. The Chandler even featured wood-weave doors to cover up the screen when not in use.

Seeing things on television was a novelty. The fact that they were live, and broadcast coast to coast, gave programs a raw thrill that has been lost today. Suspense radiated from the isolation booth of "The $64,000 Question." Led by Lucy, sitcoms were flourishing, but prime time still drew its lifeblood from burlesque, radio, and the stage. "People crowd into theaters to see their favorite radio bands," noted *Here Is Television—Your Window to the World*, published in the early 1950s, "but will they sit at their receivers and watch musicians play and singers sing?"

After Elvis, no one would think to ask that question.

"Get out in that kitchen and rattle those pots and pans!" So he sang on "Jackie Gleason's Stage Show Starring Tommy and Jimmy Dorsey" on February 11, 1956. It was the first line of "Shake, Rattle and Roll"—and probably the hottest opening in music video history. Elvis leaps on and rides the song like it is a bucking bull out of a chute. He shimmies inside his confetti-flecked oversize sports coat; his head shivers; his lips quiver. He looks ready to be catapulted off the stage.

His eyes are rolling back; he is in another world, oblivious to the camera that wobbles in on its crude dolly right up to his face. The close-up holds, but Elvis is getting shook so bad by the music that he cannot stay in the frame. He jitters out of camera range. Cut to an overhead shot, and he is absolutely possessed by the music, bent over his guitar, holding on to it and beating

it, propelled back and forth so powerfully that he barely seems to touch the floor.

The television signal is crude, the staging is primitive, the sound scratchy, the camera clumsy, and the lighting grey. But Elvis is mesmerizing. Lifelong fans will tell you that his early in-person performances were more charismatic than anything he did on television, but to see the Dorsey Brothers shows—Elvis's first national TV appearances—is to stand in awe of his ability to monopolize the camera's gaze.

Next came "The Milton Berle Show." Mr. Television, whose popularity was slipping, doesn't just let Elvis sing. He drags him into hambone comedy skits, he mugs while Elvis performs, he does the thing that adult nerds around the country must have been doing by the drove, to the dismay of their children: he imitates Elvis the Pelvis; he makes his baggy middle-age frame wiggle, and he walks on the sides of his clodhopper shoes.

Elvis chuckles charitably as Berle has his clothes torn off by fans who mistake him for their heartthrob. "Gimme the good old Rudy Vallee days," Miltie jokes. Then, resigned to what must be, he wearily calls out, "Elvis, sing your hit song," and staggers off the stage.

Elvis's growing power as a network numbers-getter awoke television critic Jack Gould of *The New York Times*, who announced that "Mr. Presley has no discernible singing ability." Gould could not contain his bile when confronted with the specter of Elvis's un-

RCA gave Elvis the big television to celebrate fifty million records sold.

Mom and Dad prepare to watch him on "The Ed Sullivan Show."

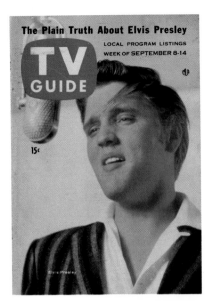

deniable success. He called his singing an "assault on the American ear" and concluded that "in the long run, perhaps Presley will do everyone a favor by pointing up the need for earlier sex education."

To the rescue of the besieged middlebrows came Steve Allen. Locked in a ratings war with Ed Sullivan, he could not ignore Elvis's proven ability to draw an audience. But Stevarino was an avowed enemy of rock and roll. So he figured out a way to beat Sullivan and neuter Elvis in one cunning swoop.

The strategy was simple. It was announced that for his July 1 appearance on "The Steve Allen Show," Elvis would not be allowed to shake. Steve would tame the Pelvis . . . and win big ratings while he was at it.

Dressed in white tie and tails, Elvis stands still and sings "Hound Dog" while petting Sherlock the basset hound, who is outfitted with a top hat. Then he is dragged though a western skit called "Range Roundup," in which he hawks "Tonto Bar" candies

("from Ptomaine, Texas"). Clichés about the Golden Age of Television do not suggest just how banal so much of it was. Allen's desperate jokes, Imogene Coca mugging like a palsy victim, Skitch Henderson leading his oleaginous orchestra: the whole show—not just Elvis— is excruciating.

Because of television, the Elvis battle was becoming a civil war. "Civilization today is sharply divided into two schools which cannot stand the sight of each other," John Lardner wrote in a *Newsweek* article about the Allen show.

WPGC radio in Washington formed "The Society for the Prevention of Cruelty to Elvis." His effigy was burned in St. Louis and hanged in Nashville, its pockets stuffed with play money.

In Wisconsin, when a radio station banned Elvis songs, a rock was thrown through its window, wrapped with a note: "I am a teenager—play Elvis Presley or we tear up the town." In Knoxville, the crew-cut football

Elvis's performance on "The Ed Sullivan Show" on January 6, 1957—when cameras dared show him only from the waist up—is now part of television folklore. It climaxed a year of network appearances that transformed a rockabilly curiosity into a nationwide cultural event.

At far left, Steve Allen introduces him to his co-star, Sherlock the basset hound. At left, Milton Berle presents a *Billboard* award for "Heartbreak Hotel." A once-dubious Ed Sullivan, finally convinced that the Atomic-Powered Singer could attract even more viewers than regular guest Topo Gigio (the Italian puppet-mouse), signed Elvis to three appearances for $50,000—more than any performer had ever been paid for a television variety show.

After Elvis sang "Hound Dog" to a basset hound on "The Steve Allen Show," the sad-eyed critter became an icon of Elvis World (as seen at right in a tinted postcard from *Jailhouse Rock,* 1957).

team pinned three long-haired Elvis look-alikes and cut off their hair.

In August, when Elvis returned to perform in Jacksonville, Florida, Reverend Gray of the Trinity Baptist Church delivered a sermon titled "Hot Rods, Reefers, and Rock and Roll," then led prayers for Elvis's salvation, declaring he had sunk to "a new low in spiritual degeneracy." Judge Marion Gooding of the Juvenile Court prepared warrants for his arrest if he moved his body in any of the dozens of ways the judge deemed threatening to the morals of minors. Police were stationed in the auditorium with 8mm movie cameras to gather evidence.

Along came Ed Sullivan, who had earlier declared, "I wouldn't have him on my show at any price." He signed Elvis for three performances, starting in September. For a recording artist in 1956 America, there was no more important venue. And for a variety show host, there was no hotter act to book.

The first time Elvis appeared, on September 9, Ed Sullivan wasn't there. Although skeptics suggested that he was playing hooky so he wouldn't have to take shrapnel when the Elvis bomb went off, Ed said he was suffering from injuries resulting from an auto accident the month before. In his place, Charles Laughton hosted "The Ed Sullivan Show."

The New York Times grudgingly gave the performance a few lines at the end of a column highlighting more momentous events, such as the beginning of National Civil Defense Week, and a "fresh, gay," new sitcom called "Hey Jeannie!" about "a wee lass [who] creates her own world of make-believe." But four out of five televisions in America had been tuned in to Elvis that night: "The Ed Sullivan Show" got the greatest numbers in ratings history, topped finally by the Beatles' appearance in 1964.

On October 28 Ed Sullivan featured Elvis for the second time, along with ventriloquist Señor Wences

(with his talking right hand) and the cast of the Broadway play *The Most Happy Fella.* When it comes time to sing ''Hound Dog''—number one on the charts since August—the audience is ripe for picking. Elvis takes his place before the camera, but holds back. He winds up with his guitar, then he pauses. Winds up again, pauses again. They are begging for him. He smiles his lopsided smile—or is it a sneer?—in complete command.

Ratings topped 80 percent, but Sullivan was getting nervous. According to the show's director, Ed believed that Elvis had attached a cardboard tube to his penis and wiggled it to make the girls scream when he sang. And so for his last appearance on the show, January 6, 1957, Elvis was reduced by strictly above-the-waist coverage to a singing bust.

But if Elvis had something funny in his pants, Ed had something even better up his sleeve. Cardboard tube or no, by keeping the scary part off-camera, the show made Elvis more lascivious than ever. You can hear the audience scream when he moves, and you *know* something wild is going on down there—limited only by your imagination. . . . And yet Ed takes credit for making Elvis decent.

After the third Sullivan appearance, Elvis's manager, Colonel Parker, raised his television price from $50,000 to $300,000. The networks said no. Elvis didn't do TV again until 1960. But that first meteoric year of exposure embedded him into America's consciousness.

It also established a pattern that lasted for his whole career. The battle to defuse him, acted out before the public on the little screen with Steve and Ed and Uncle Miltie, was a fight that would be fought time and again: with Hollywood, the Army, RCA, the Colonel. Martyrdom is one of the great mythic themes in the life of Elvis. There is always a perceived struggle between his natural, unfettered talent and all the forces that conspire to geld him.

For one year of concerts, recordings, and moviemaking after that last appearance on Ed Sullivan, Elvis reigned. But his success on national television also marked the end of what might be called the purist's dream of Elvis: Elvis the iconoclast, the small-town boy with Mom and Dad in tow. The innocence of the 1950s. The pure joy of early rock and roll. The shock and outrage among those too square to dig it.

On March 24, 1958, Elvis joined the Army. The next day, his hair was shorn. *Pageant* magazine reported, ''Fans cried, parents sighed.'' Life would never be the same for Elvis, or for the rest of the world.

Elvis and the Fall of Western Civilization

"What's most appalling is the fans' unbridled obscenity, their gleeful wallowing in smut."
—*TV Scandals*, JULY 1956

"Last night's contortionist exhibition at the Auditorium was the closest to the jungle I'll ever get."
—Helen Parmeler, Ottawa *Journal*, JULY 4, 1957

"I promise that I shall not take part in the reception accorded Elvis Presley and I shall not be present at the program presented by him at the Auditorium on Wednesday, April 3, 1957."
—Oath signed by students of the Notre Dame Convent in Ottawa (eight girls were expelled for disobeying)

"Elvis Presley's fame is a legend of the 'American Dream' of success that is overshadowed by a nightmare of bad taste. . . . His gyrations, his nose-wiping, his leers are vulgar."
—*Look*, AUGUST 7, 1956

"A new creed has been patterned by a segment of the young people of America—a creed of dishonesty, violence, lust, and degeneration."
—Cardinal Spellman, Buffalo, SEPTEMBER 30, 1956

"We do not tolerate Elvis Presley records at our dances, or blue jeans, or ducktail haircuts."
—Orren T. Freeman, principal of Wichita Falls Senior High School, FEBRUARY 24, 1957

"It is sad, but Elvis Presley has more influence on our young people than our educators."
—Jacob Potofsky, president of the Amalgamated Clothing Workers of America, regarding the blue jean fad, NOVEMBER 17, 1957

"The performance had not even the quality of true obscenity, merely an artificial and unhealthy exploitation of the enthusiasm of youth's body and mind."
—Dr. Ida Halpern, Vancouver music critic, SEPTEMBER 17, 1957

"If the agencies (TV and other) would stop handling such nauseating stuff, all the Presleys of our land would soon be swallowed up in the oblivion they deserve."
—*America: National Catholic Weekly Review*, JUNE 23, 1956

"It isn't enough to say that Elvis is kind to his parents, sends money home, and is the same unspoiled kid he was before all the commotion began. That still isn't a free ticket to behave like a sex maniac in public."
—Eddie Condon, *Cosmopolitan*, DECEMBER 1956

"The voice is a complete harangue in puffy diction and pure fervency. Under its propulsion the manufactured Folk comes to swarming life like the energetic little creatures cavorting in a hunk of rotting ham illuminated by a microscope."
—C. G. Burke, *High Fidelity*, FEBRUARY 1957

"From a strictly Marxist-Leninist viewpoint, he is a typical example of capitalist exploitation."
—*Harper's*, APRIL 1957

"Elvis Presley is morally insane. The spirit of Presleyism has taken down all the bars and standards. We're living in a day of jellyfish morality."
—The Reverend Carl E. Elgena, Des Moines, DECEMBER 3, 1956

The Other Elvis

If those who were damning him as a sexual demon could have seen how Elvis acted in private, they would have been shocked, maybe more shocked than by anything they saw onstage. How did America's number-one threat to teenage morality have fun at home? In what debauched pleasures did he wallow when he wasn't making girls faint from ecstasy?

Really, it was too silly to believe. Elvis the rebel, the bad-ass in a zoot suit, liked nothing more than splashing in his backyard pool with local kids and with his dad and cousin Junior. He liked to drink Pepsi and eat red Jell-O on the flagstone patio with his grandmother. He played with the miniature dog he had given to his mother as a present. He gathered with his parents at the piano to sing spirituals. Elvis may have seemed like a reform-school hooligan onstage, but his home life was more innocent than Beaver Cleaver's.

All his life, he lived with his family. He never left home. As he got richer and moved to bigger houses, the folks and kinfolks packed their possessions and moved up with him.

Elvis bought a pale-green ranch home at 1034 Audubon Drive in May 1956, after taking a screen test and signing a three-picture deal with Hal Wallis. He was on his way up, but his starter home was no bachelor pad or playboy sin bin. It was a decent place to share with his mother and father and beloved grandmother Minnie Mae, plus cousins, family, and friends. One of his favorite activities in the new house was sitting at the kitchen table eating cornbread dunked in buttermilk.

When the Presleys moved in, there was no fence outside, so fans gathered in the driveway to watch Elvis play in the yard, fiddle with his motorcycle, or wax his Cadillac. At night they huddled outside, pressing stethoscopes against the walls in hopes of hearing him snore. He didn't seem to mind them at all. He was grateful for the attention. If he was away on tour, girls rang the door bell and asked Gladys if she wouldn't mind wiping their hankies across the dust on *his* car or giving them a glass of water from *his* sink. The Presleys hardly ever had to mow the lawn, because the blades of grass were picked, one by one, by "Elfans" who needed them as admission to fan clubs.

The boy who furnished this home was no threat to moral order. It is a shrine to material happiness: wall-to-wall carpets, wood paneling, TV console looking out from the corner of the living room, and refrigerator full of snack foods. Couches and beds are perches for plush toys, the kind poor boys dream of winning at state fairs. Deprived all their lives of comfort, the Presleys eagerly embraced the American dream they found in Memphis department stores and furniture showrooms.

Their living room is hung with white drapes with an abstract outer-space pattern. Furniture is of the Populuxe style—overstuffed chairs with wide seats and tiny backs, so low slung and massive that they look like they could have come from the same styling studio that shaped Gladys's Sedan de Ville. There are nubby-

Memphis, 1956. As Elvis naps inside, fans gather on the lawn of his new home on Audubon Drive.

textured couches, too, a blond hi-fi, a glass coffee table, and the free-standing ash trays one finds in waiting rooms of offices.

And oh, what lamps! In every town Elvis played when he was away from home, he found a special new lamp to send back to his mother as a memento of his travels. He favored a way-out, futuristic style, with can-tilevered, split-level shades perched above gold-trimmed bases with organic shapes.

Displayed on the wood-paneled walls are warrants that make the Presleys feel proud of their good boy: a hand-tinted, illuminated publicity photograph of Elvis, "Most Promising" awards from *Cash Box* and *Billboard*, his first gold record, and a high-school diploma attesting to Elvis's "correct moral deportment."

His own bedroom is a teen retreat of floral-patterned yellow wallpaper with pink frilled fringe bedspreads. Plaster cameos of dancing muses hang above the beds; stuffed animals, white buck shoes, and a gui-

tar case share the floor. Gidget could be very happy here.

Outside, Elvis had a swimming pool dug, but he is not too sure of himself in the water and so seldom ventures into its deep end, even when Gladys vigilantly watches from the kitchen window.

It is in the wood veneer and Formica kitchen that Elvis's "one true sweetheart"—his mother—makes her son his favorite foods. Nobody can burn the bacon better than she can, or scoop the seeds out of a ripe melon, or make the thicknin' gravy to sop the biscuits in. They are best friends, Elvis and Gladys; their affection for each other is legendary. But it is a relationship with a tragic flaw.

The success she wanted for her boy took him away from her. For most of that year on Audubon Drive, as Elvis skyrocketed, Gladys and Vernon were left alone to fend off the fans and reporters. Biding time clipping articles about him from the paper for her scrapbook,

The good life, Presley style: His & Hers Cadillacs in the carport.

Dad serves iced tea on the patio.

Gladys pined for her Elvis, having premonitions of disaster, relieved only when he called—as he did each night—to reassure her he was safe. Except for the lamps he sent home as souvenirs, and his appearances on television, the boy was suddenly out of his mother's life as he had never been before. Gladys pleaded with him to settle down, get married, and open a furniture shop.

The one Christmas they spent together in the house on Audubon Drive, in 1956, Gladys and Elvis went out and bought the finest Christmas tree they could find. It was white nylon, strung with red ornaments and twinkle lights. When it was positioned in the living room, it was ringed with heaps of presents. Gladys wore her brocade frock and a Santa hat on her head. And late that night, clutching the fringed pillow Elvis had given her, the one inscribed with a sentimental poem about motherhood, she came into the pastel bedroom to tuck in the King of Rock and Roll.

When Elvis first shocked America, nothing about his cataclysmic success was more disturbing to him than the accusation by preachers that he was godless. "My mother was very upset," he told Louella Parsons about the *Life* magazine article that showed a church full of teens being taught the difference between the holy word and his music. "I had to telephone her not to worry." For his third Ed Sullivan appearance—the one on which he was shot from the waist up—his finale was a heartfelt spiritual called "Peace in the Valley" . . . after which Ed declared him a "fine and decent boy."

In 1960, *Elvis Yearbook* asked, "Ever notice how much he resembles Billy Graham?" Young fans were quoted saying that Elvis inspiration filled them when they went to church. One girl said that she believed "God sent ELVIS into this world to entertain us teen-

Elvis had what most 1950s teenage girls could only hope for:
a lovely bedroom, stuffed toys, and his very own telephone.

Top: Gladys and Vernon Presley gaze in awe at their son's first publicity picture, on the wood-panel wall of the Audubon Drive home.

Elvis's Most Famous Favorite Snack

FRIED PEANUT BUTTER AND BANANA SANDWICH

2 tablespoons smooth peanut butter
1 ripe banana, mashed
2 slices white bread
2 tablespoons margarine

Spread peanut butter and banana between slices of bread.

Melt margarine in frying pan over medium heat. Brown sandwich on both sides in melted margarine.

Serve immediately while still warm. Eat with knife and fork.

Elvis in his trailer while filming *Wild in the Country* (1960). The blue jeans are a costume. At home, he never dressed so plainly.

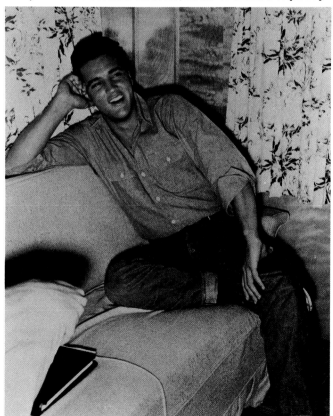

On the Elvis World calendar, Mother's Day is a high holiday. It is a time to remember
how much Elvis loved Gladys—as shown in this scrapbook sent to him by a fan.

agers." A boy wrote that "I want to have a home where God and ELVIS are the head of my family."

Religion was Elvis's lifelong companion, source not only of comfort but of his musical inspiration. The Reverend Frank Smith, his preacher back in Tupelo at the First Assembly of God Church, accompanied himself on guitar when he preached. It was in that church that Elvis, age two, left his mother's side one Sunday morning, toddling to join the choir, even though he barely knew how to talk, let alone sing.

Church was where young Elvis first connected the religious ardor of music to physical gyrations. Like the Pentacostals of today, the First Assembly of God Church in Tupelo of the 1930s was a place of uninhibited exuberance—by the preacher and his congregation. They *moved* when they sang; they wiggled, they jumped; they were seized by the same jolting, Holy Roller spirit that took hold of Elvis Presley's body when he began performing in 1954.

In Memphis (which H. L. Mencken called "the buckle on the Bible belt"), young Elvis was enraptured by the all-night gospel jubilees he heard at Ellis Auditorium. When he graduated from high school, before he got his truck-driving job at Crown Electric, he auditioned for a place among the Soul Fellows, a gospel quartet, but was rejected.

And in 1956, when Elvis the Pelvis was upsetting moralists and preachers, no one seemed to notice that he was accompanied onstage by the Jordanaires, a gospel group who opened each show by singing spirituals.

When he returned to the stage in 1969, his backups were the Imperials, then later J. D. Sumner and the Stamps—both gospel groups.

When Elvis went into the recording studio, the session regularly began with a long warm-up: Elvis at the piano, singing his favorite spirituals. Visitors to Graceland often spent their evenings listening to Elvis's extensive collection of religious records, or to Elvis himself praising God at the gold piano in his music room. Gospel music, Elvis said in *Elvis on Tour*, "puts your mind to rest. At least it does mine, since I was two."

It wasn't only in music that Elvis sought closeness with God. Throughout his life, he was obsessed with making himself righteous. He never traveled anywhere without his portable library of two hundred spiritual books, including the Bible, the Dead Sea Scrolls, *The Prophet*, and *The Impersonal Life*. When he died, he was in the bathroom reading *The Scientific Search for the Face of Jesus*. On many occasions onstage during the 1970s, when a member of the audience handed him a Bible, Elvis stopped the show and quoted favorite passages, such as the triumphs of David, the tumbling of the walls of Jericho, and the story of Creation.

He was always inquiring into religion. Buddhism, yoga, pyramid power, spiritualism: he tasted them all. He had a special fascination with Judaism. Hairdresser and spiritual advisor Larry Geller remembers finding Elvis one day in the trophy room at Graceland, sitting in a chair with the Bible in his lap, surrounded by his gold

Baby Talk

When Elvis relaxed, when he was comfortable with his most intimate friends or family, he enjoyed talking baby talk. If he really wanted to talk someone into something —especially if it was a woman—the technique was devastating.

Most of his baby talk was the kind of silly lingo that close people use to express their devotion to each other: nicknames, pet names, goofy terms for ordinary things. But like everything else he liked, he did it to extremes.

And because he did it, those around him did it too. Nearly all his associates had special names for each other, for the places and things in their world, and for the man himself, who was seldom called Elvis Presley. His retinue, known as *the Memphis Mafia*, referred to him as *Crazy* or *E* or *El* or *Big E* or *Big El* or *Tiger Man*. Stepmother Dee called him *my little Prince*. Colonel Parker virtually never said his proper name; he always referred to his client as *the Boy*. (The Colonel himself was seldom called Tom Parker; *the Colonel* was enough.)

To Priscilla, Elvis was *Fire Eyes*. To his 1970s girlfriend Linda Thompson, he was *Little Baby Buntin'*.

All members of the retinue had sobriquets. Bodyguards Red West and Sonny West were *Mr. Dragon* and *Mr. Eagle*. Charlie Hodge was *Mr. Cobra*; two-hundred-seventy-pound Lamar Fike was *Mr. Bull*, *Lardass*, or *the Wrestler*. Foreman Marty Lacker was known as *Moon*.

Alan Fortas was *Hog Ears*. James Caughley was *Hamburger James*. Karate teacher Ed Parker was *Kahuna*— Hawaiian for "high priest."

Those he loved were given special names of endearment, the supreme one being *Satinin'*, first used for Gladys, then later for Priscilla, who was also known as *'Cilla* or *Nungen* (lovey talk for "young one"). Grandmother Minnie Mae was called *Dodger*. Movie-star friend Ann-Margret was *Bunny* or *Thumper*. Anita Wood, his girlfriend in 1956, was *Little* or *Little Beady Eyes*.

As a child he called milk *butch* and water *duckling*. Marian Cocke, his nurse at Baptist Memorial Hospital in the 1970s, taught him to call Pepsi-Cola *bellywash*. He told her to *lather* his coffee (add cream and sugar) for breakfast, then followed it with vast quantities of banana pudding spooned straight from the serving bowl. Other than 'naner pudding, his favorite dessert was *iddytream* (ice cream); and among his favorite nursery foods were *soaks*—hunks of cornbread sopped in buttermilk.

Presents were *happies*; works of art were *pretties*. Dainty women's feet were known as *sooties*.

In moments of great emotion, it was baby talk that best expressed the happy innocence of his feelings. "Nungen," he whispered to Priscilla when Lisa Marie was born, "us has a baby girl."

The Teens' Angel

From the time he was six years old and gave his new tricycle to a child even poorer than him, Elvis was possessed by an unquenchable desire to do good. Moralists saw him only as a rock and roll hellion; but legions of fans knew that Elvis—church raised, mother loving, and deferent to his elders—was a saint.

In those same turbulent years when he was wreaking musical havoc in auditoriums coast to coast, charities harnessed his charismatic energy to do battle against disease and misfortune. He fought cancer with a check-up, a check, and a tumor-defying sneer. He donated truckloads of teddy bears to victims of infantile paralysis and was named "King of Hearts" when he launched a "Teens vs. Polio" campaign. At right, he

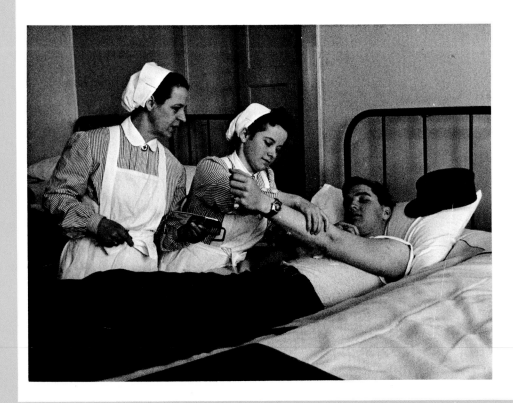

gives March of Dimes Girl Joanne Wilson of Rockaway Beach, New York, a big lollipop (1/7/57). He got his own Salk shot just before his second appearance on "The Ed Sullivan Show" (10/28/56).

While filming *Jailhouse Rock*, he was visited at MGM Studios by polio victims Beth Currier and Diane Brackway, who shared their Elvis scrapbook with their hero.

Even those unimpressed by his good deeds could not deny the virtue of GI Elvis, who insisted he be treated like any other draftee during basic training and his tour of duty overseas. At far left, German nurses find proof that he is a red-blooded American boy.

records. He was weeping. When Larry asked why, Elvis explained, "Because I'm not Jewish." He felt slighted not to be one of the chosen people. When Elvis served as best man at his buddy George Klein's wedding, he echoed every word the rabbi said, becoming so enthusiastically involved in the ceremony that he started getting ahead of the rabbi! "If it had been possible," Marty Lacker wrote, "I really believe Elvis would have officiated."

At one point in the 1960s, when he began feeling troubled by the meaninglessness of movies like *Tickle Me* and *Girl Happy*, he announced to Larry Geller that he had decided to put an end to it all by joining a monastery. Larry tried to imagine Elvis wearing a monk's robe. He also imagined how Colonel Parker would take the news that his meal ticket was planning to go into gardening on God's behalf . . . and quickly talked Elvis out of it.

In *Elvis and Me*, Priscilla Presley recalled her frustrations living with Elvis in Bel-Air during the 1960s. What she wanted was romance. On the other hand, Elvis wanted to hold Bible readings for his female fans. As girls in their "lowest cut blouses and shortest miniskirts" listened in rapt attention, their idol preached long into the night.

By the end of his career, he stood center stage and unfurled his faith without pause or embarrassment. Like Kate Smith blasting out "God Bless America," he brought audiences to their feet singing of God and country. "Glory, glory, hallelujah!" he rejoiced during concerts in his operatic "American Trilogy."

Even in those mid-1970s shows when you can hear that he is tired, walking uninspired through the rock and roll, he is suddenly exalted when he launches into the gospel song "How Great Thou Art." His voice soars. It is not so surprising, when one feels the bone-shaking passion in these religious arias, that all three of the Grammys he won were for sacred songs.

Listen: This is not just any god he is singing to; it is —in Elvis's emphatic phrasing—MY God, a being with whom the singer truly believes he has a close personal relationship. At a time when John Lennon was boasting that the Beatles were more popular than Jesus, Elvis was happy to take second place behind his Lord. Perhaps he was too modest: "I have often wondered," Elvis biographer Patsy Hammontree quotes a fan describing a concert, "would it have been any different if Christ himself were there?"

alo, Everybody, Halo," *Variety* headlined in September 1956. "There is talk of accenting Presley's church-going family background," the article reported, in order to "re-create the rock 'n' roller into an influence for the good."

To prove to the world that he was a nice guy, Elvis went on publicity dates. Yvonne Lime, a pert ponytailer with a button nose who had played a small part in *Loving You*, revealed what he was really like in a diary excerpt called "My Weekend with Elvis" in *Modern Screen*.

Elvis, she rhapsodizes, called her every night in Hollywood, pleading that she visit him at home. The reason was, of course, that he wanted his mother, Gladys, to meet Yvonne—the first step in any relationship he had with a girl. Friends advised her against going to see him, warning that he was fickle. "How could I tell anyone how sincere and lonely Elvis sounded?" she wondered. On Friday of Easter weekend, she flew to Memphis.

He was waiting for her at the airport in his shiny pink Caddy. Graceland was being renovated, so they went to the house on Audubon Drive. Shocked by how small it seemed, Yvonne had to circumnavigate rooms crowded with furniture Elvis had bought and cartons full of fan mail (half of it addressed to Gladys) that the besieged family couldn't figure out how to dispose of.

Gladys greeted Yvonne at the door and put a motherly arm around her. "We want you to feel at home here, dear."

Then Elvis took her to his bedroom. And what did the twosome do in there? They admired his teddy bears and stuffed animals, and she gave him a little toy chicken with a little red cap on its head. Elvis put the chick in the place of honor, bowed, then kissed Yvonne on the tip of her nose.

That first night of their date they ate meat loaf and mashed potatoes at the family dinner table, Elvis explaining that he preferred meat loaf to steak because it was quicker to eat.

Afterwards, Yvonne wanted to dance the bop, but Elvis wasn't feeling well. He had a skin rash. So he and his parents and Yvonne all sat outside in lawn chairs enjoying the evening breeze. With Gladys on one side and Yvonne on the other, Elvis took both their hands and sighed tenderly, "My two best girls!"

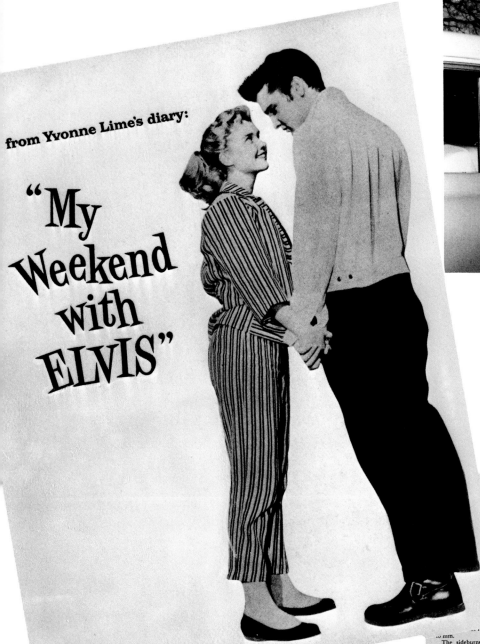

from Yvonne Lime's diary:

"My Weekend with ELVIS"

dence, his rejection of conformity to the environment which at the same time nursed him and stifled him. Perhaps he was kicking out blindly, as an infant kicks aside its swaddling clothes. And perhaps he held on to them against ridicule for the same reason that many mature nonconformists grow beards.

While he and his friends played in the streets and stood on corners, the big, shiny, rich world rolled by in big, shiny, rich cars. All right, he wasn't big and he wasn't rich, but by gosh he could grow sideburns if he wanted to.

Perhaps he was a rebel with a cause he didn't fully

an do about it. Sometimes some-
change your whole appearance."
Elvis can't take any chances. A
nt printed pictures of Elvis with
n."

rom Elvis's fans came a thunder-

mind your own business. We
," was one typical response in a

lvis' old friends from Humes
was in school Elvis used to
ng about those sideburns. He
much, tho. He was regular,

Memphis State College re-
a study of Elvis' personality,
ss from what they knew of
und.

his desire to be himself is
nm. It has been both helpful and harmful

The sideburns were his declaration of indepen-

"Hamburgers—I love 'em!"
—Elvis prefers a hamburger
to the finest steak.

"Plain ice water!"
—Elvis never touches alcohol and
never smokes.

It was easy for teen magazines to depict the nice side of Elvis. No press agent was needed to embroider these facts: Elvis lived at home, introduced all his dates to his mother, and didn't drink. He read the Bible, collected teddy bears, and liked girls who were virgins.

Saturday night, they went to a party at record producer Sam Phillips's house. Elvis had to leave because his rash was worse, so he and Yvonne went to the hospital, where he got some penicillin to clear it up. Feeling better, he insisted they return to the party.

It was late. It was raining. Many of the guests had left. The few remaining revelers gathered on the floor in the darkened living room, illuminated only by the flickering fire. "It was a thrilling experience," Yvonne writes. What was the big thrill? "Elvis began to sing a religious song." He sang the "hymns and spirituals he loves so well . . . on and on, until day began to break and it was Easter morning."

At dawn the partyers topped off their merriment with scrambled eggs, cooked just the way Elvis liked them: "hard as a rock."

Fan-magazine stories of "girls who got to Elvis" tell variations of the same wholesome boy. With Anita Wood, he went shopping for Christmas presents (and wrapped her pearl-encrusted watch in paper made of hundred-dollar bills). With June Juanico, it was horseback riding down in Biloxi. For big dates, Elvis splurged, but not on fancy restaurants or sophisticated nightclubs. He rented the Fairgrounds Amusement Park so he and his date and his pals could ride the dodge-'em cars, or the Rainbow Roller Rink, where they could play crack the whip and eat pronto pups dipped in mustard.

When starlet Dotty Harmony was brought to Graceland to meet Gladys, she stayed two weeks. It was because of Elvis, she told *Screenland* magazine, that she quit smoking ("That's a good girl," he said when she crushed out her last cigarette); and she stopped having even an occasional glass of wine. Elvis told her of the "many lives he had seen ruined by drink."

Dotty also noticed how "all his tensions fell away" when he was around Gladys. Mother and son were always kissing and touching. "He was wild about her coconut cake and corn bread." *Screenland* wondered in the article, titled "Elvis Presley's Marriage Dilemma": How could he ever find a girl to match his mother?

The ultimate proof of Elvis's character came during the Army years. Taken away from his home for the first time in his life, he was torn between his desire to be a good soldier and his devotion to his mother. Although his career had wedged

Hollywood newcomer: Elvis is welcomed by the MGM messenger girl corps in 1956.

between them, Gladys and Elvis had never been so dramatically apart; and although the press focused on his sudden reduction from superstar to GI Joe, the real drama was his immense separation anxiety.

"Star is Shorn," gloated *Life*, describing how Private Presley was "advanced $7 on his month's pay of $78." He was paraded like a dog in the show ring so the press could record every inoculation, every measurement, and, of course, the famous haircut (with Elvis muttering, "Hair today, gone tomorrow"). A special detail was assigned to sweep and destroy all clippings.

He looks extraordinarily vulnerable: pale, hairless, and naked except for a pair of Jockey shorts. He had arrived in a Cadillac with a cute blonde and left in the Army bus, struggling under the weight of his duffel bag.

More than her son, Gladys was flattened by the separation. After he completed basic training at Fort Hood in Texas, he moved her and his father and his cousins to a house in nearby Killeen. But it was too late. The golden cord between him and Gladys had been severed. Dark circles underneath her eyes foretold the end.

For Elvis, basic training was a piece of cake. He had done fine in ROTC in high school. He obeyed orders just like any conscientious soldier. What hurt was being away from home.

He did what he could to make his new surroundings seem familiar. He hung around with Eddie Fadal, a disc jockey he had met in 1956. Eddie and his wife added a room to their house in Waco, where Elvis could come relax on leave. It was done up in Elvis's favorite color scheme—pink and black—and Eddie gave him keys to his Lincoln Continental. Elvis played touch football with neighborhood kids and celebrated birthday parties and drank milk at the kitchen table (which he much preferred to the formal dining room).

Despite Eddie's support and that of Master Sergeant Bill Norwood (who comforted Elvis when he broke down and cried from homesickness), the Presley family was disintegrating. *This* was the true horror of the Army years—not the haircut, not the discipline, not the hiatus in his career.

Gladys's health was failing. She worried frantically about her boy, fretting how the sound of cannon fire would hurt his delicate musician's ears, and how Killeen was nowhere near as nice as Memphis. On August 14, she succumbed to hepatitis, complicated by a weak heart and a dependency on liquor that had not soothed the ache of her absent son at all. Obituaries listed her age as forty-two. (She was actually forty-six.)

Elvis was on leave, sleeping at Graceland, when Vernon called with the news. Cousin Billy Smith took the call and told the boy his mother was dead. He fell apart. Accounts of his emotional state as he grieved are almost unbearable to hear. He threw himself on her coffin, weeping over her tiny feet, calling her by the baby-talk names they had used in private conversation. He caressed her lifeless body, combing its hair, wailing laments as he clutched her pink housecoat (the one he had given her) to his chest. He talked to the corpse, telling it which visitors had come to pay their respects. No one, no relatives or friends, not even his father, could penetrate the delirium that engulfed Elvis in his moment of abysmal pain.

"I lived my whole life for you!" he cried out at the cemetery. "Everything I have is gone," he moaned as he fell upon the casket, releasing tidal waves of sorrow that embarrassed those in attendance unfamiliar with the physical agitation that often accompanied services

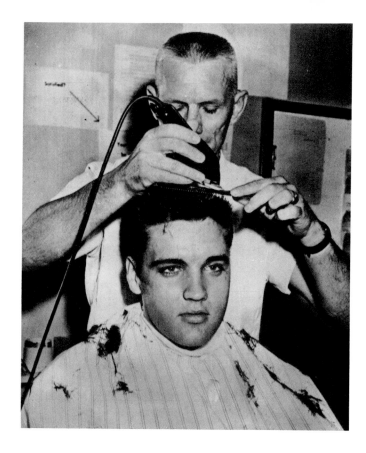

In 1958, Elvis lost it all. A draft notice halted his career at its zenith. The famous hair was mowed to a GI stubble. Then, on August 14, his mother, Gladys, died at age forty-six.

and wakes in the Church of God. He grieved like he sang—racked with emotion, oblivious to the judgments of others.

What a surreal vision of hell it must have been for Elvis. His mother—the one woman who knew how to comfort him—was gone; but legions of would-be Gladyses—fans who wanted fiercely to mother him—swarmed the cemetery and Graceland gates, fighting to be by his side.

What did they know about his real fears? About the nightmares and sleepwalking and insomnia that had haunted him since childhood? The boy who never left home in all his twenty-three years could now never go home. For hours, he stood outside Graceland looking up at the white-columned porch of the dream house he had bought for his mother. He spent nine days locked in his bedroom while the world waited, camera ready.

After Gladys died, Elvis was shipped to Germany. Holding a copy of *Poems That Touch the Heart,* he sailed from Brooklyn as the Army band played "All Shook Up." At Graceland, the windowpane against which Gladys fell when she was stricken remained broken. Elvis ordered that it not be repaired, and that all her clothes and personal effects remain exactly where they were when she left the house for the last time.

He brought his father and grandmother and his buddies Red West and Lamar Fike to Germany, and tried to make a normal life in a house in Bad Nauheim,

Germany, 1959. Elvis hugs his grandma (second from right) and two of her pals.

where he would go whenever he wasn't on the base. It was furnished just like an American home, with televisions, a piano, and a refrigerator stocked with hamburger meat, bacon, and brown 'n' serve rolls. But Elvis didn't have a good time when he was stationed in Germany. He was raw with grief, numbed by the forced separation from everything that made him feel secure. There were only a few nights out, one trip to Paris, a two-week leave in Munich. Mostly, the boy did his duty and he stayed at home. No soldier was ever more obedient to his country and his kin.

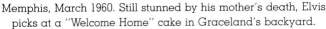

Memphis, March 1960. Still stunned by his mother's death, Elvis picks at a "Welcome Home" cake in Graceland's backyard.

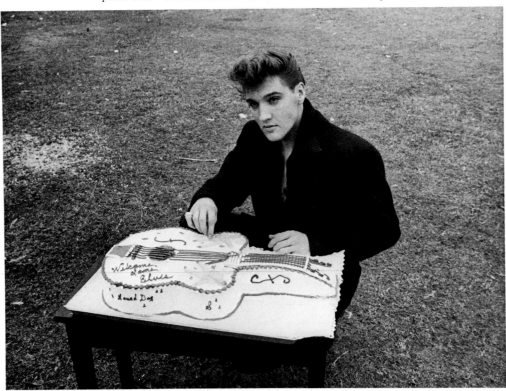

Celluloid Elvis

Elvis Presley movies": they are a genre all by themselves. Who cannot conjure up their bright, familiar features: Elvis serenading pretty girls; Elvis zooming somewhere in a sporty car; Elvis frolicking on the beach; Elvis kissing and laughing his way through a Technicolor world as sweet and blubbery as Jell-O.

To understand the emergence of Celluloid Elvis, you have to know how much he wanted to be a movie star. Music—his first love—came easy. He sang with his family, at home, in church. It was natural to practice singing, stretch his voice, explore new kinds of songs. But making movies was a distant dream—a big part of his dream of stardom.

As a high-school boy, he ushered at the Loew's State Theater, memorizing lines from *King Solomon's Mines* and *The Prince Who Was a Thief*. He was held in thrall by movies that were bigger than life and movie stars who were heroes. How glorious the celluloid world must have looked to the poor boy sweltering in Lauderdale Courts Housing Project. Life on the big screen was one of adventure, wealth, glamour, and happy endings. The women were beautiful and pure. The men were handsome and strong. Goodness triumphed. And what power movie stars had over their audience!

Think of Elvis the sixteen-year-old Memphian who had never known anything but the powerlessness of poverty. Movies were his escape. To star in them would be to have the status of a god.

At first it looked as though he might travel the same mean street to movie stardom that he had gone with rock and roll. The pre-Army pictures bristle with the insolence of his early music. They are rough and raw, and alive with promise that he could indeed develop the acting skills to convey the sensual vitality of his singing.

When he accuses Cathy (Debra Paget) of being a whore in *Love Me Tender* (1956), he does it with the same explosive anger that powered his singing in "Blue Suede Shoes." The sleazy New Orleans world he inhabits in *King Creole* (1958) is as nasty as any of his rock and roll lyrics. Although he was still rough around the edges as an actor, Elvis Presley took to playing a rebel every bit as much as he relished singing like one.

There are great moments in *Loving You* (1957) that trade on early Elvis as an icon of naughtiness. The movie parallels his career and allows him to act out scenes with fans, promoters, and fellow musicians and to stands up onstage, within the film, and perform as Elvis. He is a tough character—sullen, short tempered, unwilling to take crap from anybody.

Jailhouse Rock, the story of a surly singer-convict on his way to the top, evokes all the juicy moral ambiguity that Elvis Presley represented to America in 1957. The "Jailhouse Rock" dance number, choreographed by Elvis, is one of the high-water marks of his career—yet another glimmer of potential never fully realized. Elvis stands up, faces the camera, and announces the song. Then hell breaks loose—a red-hot musical number free of the strangleholds of character and plot.

Before they drifted into a happy-go-lucky routine of pretty songs and girl salads, Elvis movies had hair on their chests. In *Jailhouse Rock* (far right) he played a punk with an attitude. But by *Kid Galahad* in 1962, despite a Brandoesque undershirt, his character was flawless. Runaway success of the frolicsome *Blue Hawaii* (1961) replaced rock-and-roll rebellion with seven years of movie-matinee exasperation.

He hit Hollywood like a double whammy of Brando and Marilyn Monroe. "Elvis Can Act!" announced reviews of *Jailhouse Rock* and *King Creole*. The Atomic-Powered Singer was a natural candidate for the 1950s pantheon of antiheros. There was talk of his starring in the James Dean story; of his working with Nicholas Ray, director of *Rebel Without a Cause* and specialist in movies about alienation.

But when he came back from the Army, everything changed. "The Elvis Presley everyone thinks he is— isn't," *Life* noted in 1960 in an article about his forthcoming movies. "He is no longer the sneering, hip-swinging symbol of the untamed beast that resides in 17-year-old breasts."

He had no intention of returning to the live concert performances that had given the country conniption fits. Nor did he want his film career to reflect the devilish side of rock and roll. "I don't know how long the music end of it will last," he said, hoping to concentrate instead on his goal of becoming a movie star. He never lost his love of music; but neither did Elvis ever give up wanting to show the world he could act.

He tried extraordinarily hard to do well in Hollywood. It is said that Michael Curtiz, director of *King Creole*, didn't want to work with Elvis, and therefore tried making impossible demands on the allegedly undisciplined newcomer. During pre-production, Curtiz mentioned that Elvis looked too plump. Elvis crash-dieted and lost ten pounds in the next two weeks.

He told Hal Kanter, writer-director of *Loving You*, that he intended not to smile when he acted because he had studied the greats--Bogart, Brando, Dean—and realized that they seldom smiled. He was a perfectionist who demanded retakes even if the director was satisfied. But he was never seen as a prima donna. "I recall how especially courteous he was," said Ina Balin (leading lady in *Charro!* [1969]). "In the hurry-up world of Hollywood, his southern manners made an impression."

Elvis was an odd duck by the standards of Hollywood. Natalie Wood, his steady girl for a while, was shocked by the way he behaved. She was accustomed to fast-track movie stars, wild parties, nonconformist behavior. Elvis's idea of a great date was a trip to the malt shop for cheeseburgers. He was a sex symbol who acted like a choirboy.

The post-Army movies—approved, commissioned, and controlled by Colonel Tom Parker—were perfect vehicles for this angelic fellow. "I'll play it my way," he declares in *G.I. Blues* (1960), his first movie after coming home: "nice, clean, wholesome."

At first, there were exceptions: *Flaming Star* (1960)

Elvis electrified *Jailhouse Rock* (above) with the corybantic frenzy of his concerts. While filming *Love Me Tender* (right), he tried to teach the crew to shake, rattle, and roll.

and *Wild in the Country* (1961). Both were serious roles . . . but neither movie could compete with the box office generated by *Blue Hawaii* (1961) (originally titled *Beach Boy*), which established Elvis's escapist formula.

Perhaps the singer of "Blue Suede Shoes" had a future as the next James Dean; but the other Elvis, the mama's boy with malt-shop good manners, was much better served by movies that were morally impeccable.

One fact is constant in every post-Army Elvis movie: his virtuous character. He is never corrupt. Barbra Streisand offered him the co-starring role in her version of *A Star Is Born*. It was a chance at a serious meat-on-the-bones acting role; but it was turned down. Colonel Parker wanted too much money; plus Elvis could never play a weak-willed alcoholic, let alone a has-been. Director Norman Taurog said he wanted to find a story in which Elvis played a cold-blooded killer: the Colonel wouldn't hear of it. Bob Mitchum wanted him for a 1960 remake of *Thunder Road;* but there was no way that Elvis—who idolized highway patrolmen—would play a bootlegger outrunning the law.

No major sins were allowed in Elvis Presley movies. With rare exceptions, he didn't cheat, he didn't lie, he didn't steal, he didn't fornicate, drink, or swear. Little transgressions were fine: white lies, necking and light petting, double entendres.

Instead of moral dilemmas or profound life crises, Elvis movies present their star with annoyances. He is fired because he kisses a girl *(Paradise, Hawaiian Style* [1966]*);* he is bugged by his parents to join the family pineapple business *(Blue Hawaii* [1961]*);* he runs out of gas *(Follow That Dream* [1962]*).* These irritating situations make him a wee bit alienated, a condition he expresses by wrinkling his forehead often. "Something is always happening to me," said Elvis, describing his movie roles. "Someone's always telling me what to do."

"It's Elvis barrelin', bikin', and bikini-ing and belting out the wild Presley beat." "See Elvis where the fun never sets!" "See Elvis make the beach a ball!" "Watch Elvis sing and swing and give the bikini-clad beauties and the girl-happy guys a rompin', rockin' good time." That is how his movies were sold: ninety minutes of Elvis goofing around in front of the camera—nothing less, nothing more.

Madcap Elvis finds himself in one wacky situation after another, surrounded by beach bunnies doing the frug and cookie-faced tykes whose diapers he must change. What adventures he has! Fists fly out at him as soon as he enters a bar. He falls off trapezes; leopards

MGM publicity releases describe *Live a Little, Love a Little* (1968) as a racy romantic comedy in which Elvis leads "a life of constant defeat, disaster, and defense." The humiliation begins when he is chased into the ocean by a dog. He then contracts pneumonia, gets drugged by a girl who wants his body, is fired from his job, loses his apartment, suffers night terrors, and—in a rare occurrence for an Elvis movie—goes all the way . . . after which his paramour runs away. Much of the movie's fun is in seeing Elvis race frantically between two bosses who are enemies, one demanding he be a square, the other requiring he be a hipster. At left, he stands dumbfounded by his new assignment as a glamour photographer. Below, he is harassed by Albert the Great Dane. *Live a Little, Love a Little* was adapted from Dan Greenburg's novel *Kiss My Firm But Pliant Lips.*

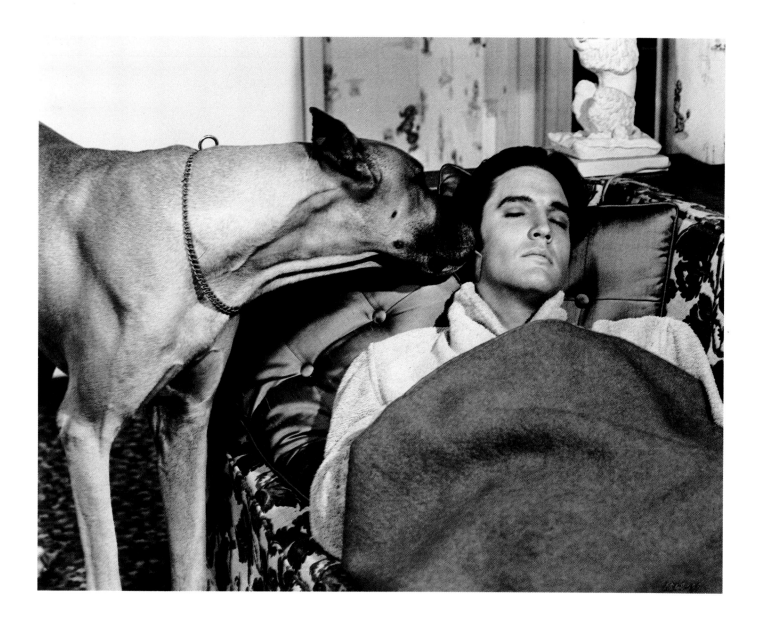

leap out of trees only to meet a devastating Elvis karate chop that sends them to cat heaven. He confronts deep-sea fish, overdone pot roasts, and the IRS. He dives off cliffs a hundred and thirty feet high. He is chased by Scotland Yard, by gangsters, by con men, by posses, and by pirates after sunken treasure. If he sits down to relax between adventures, he gets right up to sing "Cotton Candy Land" or "Vino, Dinero, y Amor."

"These are Elvis Presley pictures," *Time* quoted an MGM executive. "They don't need titles. They could be numbered." Until the formula pooped out, they did great box office, averaging $5 million gross apiece (and costing about one-tenth that to produce).

When critics reviewed them, they were bothered by deficiencies of plot and character. But such traditional dramatic values are irrelevant to Elvis Presley movies.

It is the lesser works—pictures like *Double Trouble* (1967), *Girls! Girls! Girls!* (1962), and *Harum Scarum* (1965)—that are a revelation. These movies—the bottom-of-the-barrel Elvis pix, the worst of the lot—are paradoxically the most modern. They are the precursors of music video. There is little essential difference, after all, between Elvis in *Blue Hawaii* and Mick Jagger prancing around in the video version of "Harlem Shuffle," surrounded by sultry women and surreal scenery. When one views a music video, one does not compare it to narrative cinema. It is a different kind of film language.

One long, glorious scene in *Paradise, Hawaiian Style* suggests how the elements of the Elvis Presley Movie Formula are aimed at creating Perfect Elvis Moments rather than serving the story. It is a musical number called "Drums of the Islands," an extravaganza in which Elvis sails on a South Seas war canoe among a crowd of islanders. They stand on shore waving and he waves back; girls in grass skirts shimmy, old men toot conch shells, young men up to their ears in leis flex their muscles.

Elvis keeps floating past, the music builds, the camera pulls back in a majestic aquatic track to reveal hundreds more hip-swiveling, drum-pounding natives. All the fanfare is for Elvis. And when he is delivered on shore like a landbound Esther Williams, he leads the entire grass-skirt island chorus in song and dance.

Why the Elvis apotheosis? His character in the movie is nothing more than a guy who runs a helicopter taxi service. So how come the natives are offering up their finest ceremony to him? There is scant explanation in the plot ("Want to take a ride on the canoe?"), but by this point in his motion picture career, none is called for. All that matters is that he is ELVIS, and this is an ELVIS MOVIE; therefore, all eyes are focused on his radiant beauty. It is a moment of cinematographic free fall, a revelation of what Elvis Presley movies are really all about. When the exuberance ends and Elvis is sucked back into the zombie life of his character, Rick Richards, one waits impatiently for the next song, when Elvis will bloom again like a great synthetic flower.

These movies were loved in the Third World even

sings "Clambake." Put him inside a colorful south-of-the-border bar and you have *Fun in Acapulco* (1963). Get out the turban and he'll do an Arabian cha-cha in *Harum Scarum*. Watch him zoom fast in *Speedway* (1968) and *Spinout* (1966). See Elvis water-ski, ride a horse and a motorcycle and a rickshaw, fly a helicopter, kiss a girl.

You could have ever so much fun watching Elvis do many interesting things in many pretty places; but the movies were not allowed to show Elvis die. When word got out that he was going to get shot at the end of *Love Me Tender*, fans were furious. They picketed theaters. They petitioned 20th Century–Fox, pleading for a reprieve. In response, Elvis was filmed in close-up sing-

Fans liked him dressed as a sheik (above in *Harum Scarum*) and a prizefighter (right in *Kid Galahad*), but they could not swallow his on-screen death in *Love Me Tender* (far right).

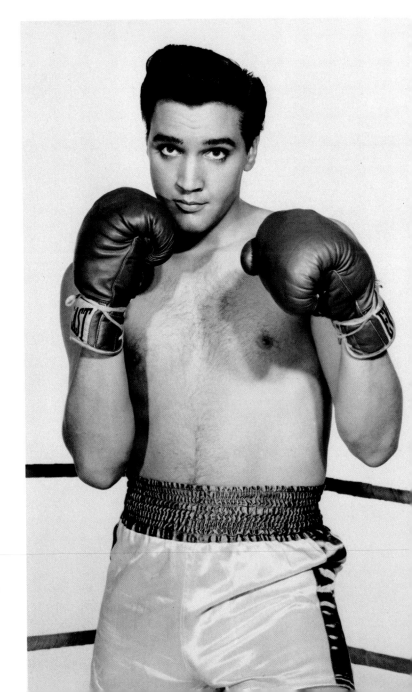

more than in America. "The sixties," writes Nitaya Kanchanawan of Ramkhamhaeng University in Bangkok, "were the best time for Elvis in Thailand. His kind of movies fit the idea of Thai entertainment. . . . People were happy when they left the theater. The Thais love to see 'beautiful things' and listen to 'beautiful sounds.'"

What a shame that Elvis didn't have a Busby Berkeley or Mitchell Leisen to infuse his gaudy celluloid world with the vim of a "Broadway Melody" or an *Easy Living*! In the 1930s, Elvis might have been a supreme icon of Hollywood studio grandeur; in the 1980s, of music-video razzle-dazzle. But movies of the 1960s didn't have the style; musicals were dead, genres were dying. Compared with the artiness of the decade's celebrated films such as *Bonnie and Clyde* or *Easy Rider*, Elvis pictures were fluff. And fluff was taboo in earnest 1960s America.

In retrospect, the best way to understand them is to see Elvis Presley movies as the cinematic equivalent of playing dolls. Dress Elvis up in a sailor's outfit and he

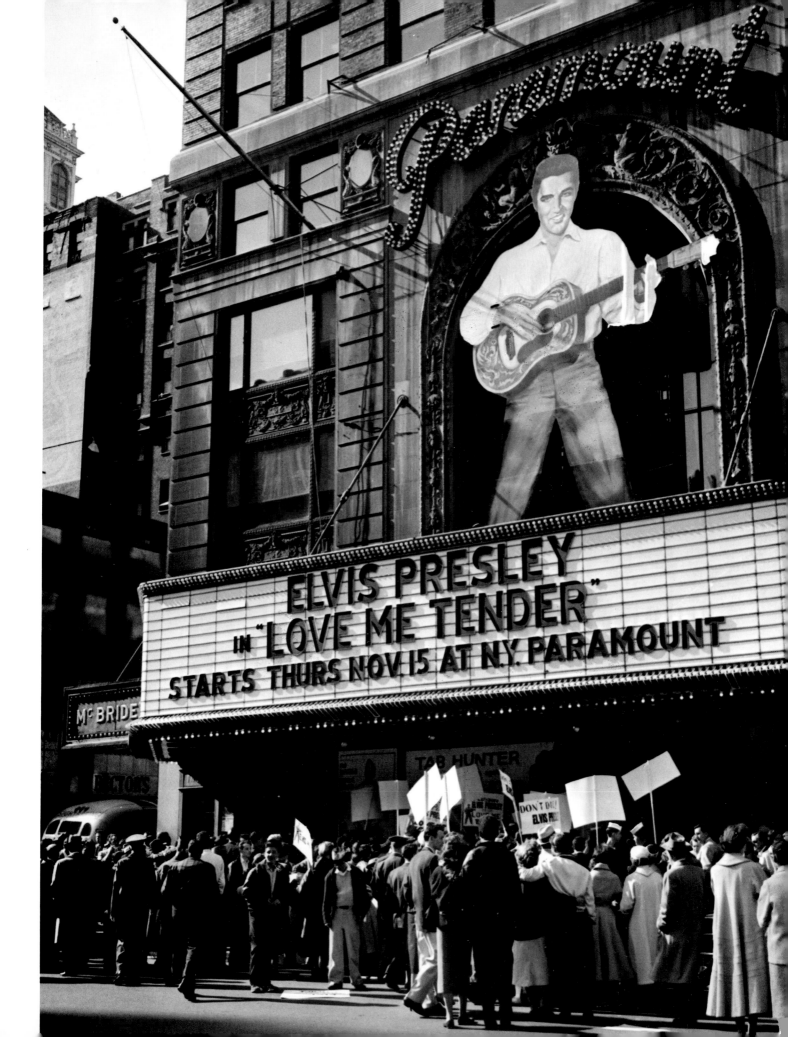

ing the title song and his face was superimposed over the final scene in the film. Nonetheless, he was dead. Fans wept. When his mother, Gladys, saw it, she was upset for days.

The last feature film he made, *Change of Habit* (1969), was a wild game for the Elvis doll to play. Here he is dressed as a mod ghetto doctor, in love with the Mary Tyler Moore doll, named Sister Michelle, who is dressed as a plainclothes nun. To put a point on this merry little parenthesis, observe the credit sequence— in which three nuns do a slow striptease, in body-parts close-ups, removing their habits and lisle stockings, then dressing themselves in miniskirts and go-go boots, while Elvis sings "Change of Habit."

It is said that Elvis was terribly frustrated by his movie career, that he disliked some of the scenes he had to play so much that he became physically ill. *Charro!* (in which he doesn't shave) and *Change of Habit* (in which he tries to cure society's ills) suggest new directions for his screen character. But Elvis never broke out of the matinee idol ghetto in which Hollywood had trapped him.

Why didn't he quit sooner? Inertia; easy money; bad advice by Colonel Parker: all likely explanations. After all, the movies earned him at least $3 million per year; during the first half of the 1960s, he was among the top box-office attractions in America. Consider also the Other Elvis, and how compliance with these movies was true to his nature.

Consider that once he got up onstage to perform in 1955, he never sat down again. He was bombarded by the magnitude of his fame, ugly criticism, and the loss of his mother. He was a simple boy who suddenly found himself an international sex symbol. Life was complicated for Elvis Presley. Most of his post-Army movies are no more complicated than a smiling yellow happy face. As in a pro wrestling match, they have moral values you can see. Good guys win the girl. Good guys have fun. People like them.

Elvis knew that life wasn't like that. He had lived a reality far stranger than what any script writer could invent. But the movies were a haven—as they had been when he was sixteen years old and watching them from the audience—where things work out as they should before "The End" appears.

True fans continue to love Elvis movies for reasons beyond film critics' intellectual grasp. Despite all the overwrought excuses given for his ten-year motion-picture career, and even despite his own growing dissatisfaction with Hollywood, the Elvis Presley filmography is

Elvis the movie star cheerfully assumed the duties of celebrity. Below, at an awards banquet before a 1961 charity concert in Memphis, he poses with clubwomen and gift-wrapped RCA Nippers. At right, in a publicity picture from *Live a Little, Love a Little*, he strums and smiles into the business end of Rudy Vallee's megaphone. Like Elvis, Rudy had begun as an overwhelmingly successful popular singer.

a very real expression of the character of a man who for his whole life wanted to maintain a child's wide-eyed vision of the world.

The painful thing about Elvis's movie career is what it did to his music. For most of the 1960s, all he sang were soundtrack songs: three albums and four singles each year. Between 1960 and 1968, Elvis didn't appear once on the country charts. With the exception of "Devil in Disguise" in 1963, he vanished from the R&B charts. He didn't have a number-one single between "Good Luck Charm" (1962) and "Suspicious Minds" (1969). The man who once shook the nation by belting out "Hound Dog" and "Heartbreak Hotel" in auditoriums from coast to coast spent nearly a decade in Hollywood singing cheerful bromides such as "Fort Lauderdale Chamber of Commerce" and "No Room to Rhumba in a Sports Car."

What happened? Partly, the change was Elvis's choice. When he walked into Sun Studios in 1954, he had no intention of becoming a rock and roller. He wanted to be a ballad singer, and began by imitating Dean Martin. His biggest post-Army hit, in 1960, was

"It's Now or Never"—an operatic update of "O sole mio," the Neapolitan song that Caruso had first cut in 1916.

The other reason for his recession was the changing nature of the music business. In the 1950s, when Elvis was super-hot, songwriters who wanted him to sing their material had to sign a percentage of the writer's profits over to a Presley publishing company under the umbrella of Hill and Range Music Publishers. Because he was Elvis, the King of Rock and Roll, good composers such as Otis Blackwell ("Don't Be Cruel") and Leiber and Stoller ("Jailhouse Rock") were willing to do it. Elvis was on the cutting edge when he sang material such as "Heartbreak Hotel" (written especially for him by Mae Boren Axton and Tommy Durden), Carl Perkins's "Blue Suede Shoes," and Charles Calhoun's "Shake, Rattle and Roll." It is with such songs he made his early reputation.

But in the 1960s, the music business was a-changin'—ironically, thanks in large part to the rock revolution Elvis inspired. More singers were writing their own songs, turning popular music into a political statement, taking for themselves the creative power once held by the music publishing companies. Elvis, on the other hand, never wrote a song in his life. He did produce all his songs (unofficially), but his real art was singing, which began to seem less important in the issue-oriented 1960s. The innocence of rock and roll was being usurped by songs heavy with messages and meanings. Bob Dylan and the Beatles were making history by writing as well as performing songs that became anthems of a cultural revolution.

Meanwhile, Elvis required tons of original material to fill his contractual obligation for three soundtrack albums per year. It was not profitable to include covers of other singers' hits in movies, and the composer's guild in Hollywood didn't permit members to write on spec. So it was up to Hill and Range to provide it all. They distributed Elvis movie scripts to their stable of writers, with places marked where songs were needed. And the Tin Pan Alley composers obliged, writing songs perfectly suited to movies like *Girls! Girls! Girls!* and *Paradise, Hawaiian Style*. They had Elvis singing "Queenie Wahine's Papaya" and "Yoga Is as Yoga Does." Compared with other leading 1960s pop stars, the King of Rock and Roll began to seem as corny as Lawrence Welk. Nobody hated this predicament more than Elvis himself.

Then in 1968 he turned his career around with a dramatic flourish nearly comparable to the first shock of 1956.

One of the greatest events in Elvis World history is the comeback of 1968. It is a story of rebirth, of kicking free from all that had strangled and suppressed him for a decade. At the heart of the story is Colonel Tom Parker.

The Colonel first entered Elvis's life in 1955. Elvis was making a regional name for himself playing small clubs and auditoriums in the South. Parker, whose background included touring with carnivals, where he made chickens dance to "Turkey in the Straw" by standing them on hotplates, had elevated himself to booking concerts for country and western singers Hank Snow and Eddy Arnold.

Within months of their getting together, Elvis hit big. The Colonel's exclusive contract earned him 25 percent of everything his boy made (and in its final draft in 1967, *half*).

In the beginning, Elvis didn't make a move without Colonel Parker's approval. They seemed like a perfect pair, each outrageous in his own venue—Elvis up on-

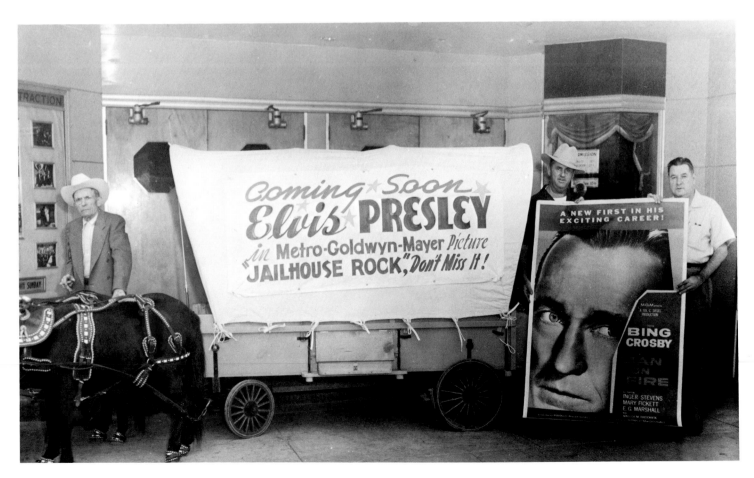

stage diddling the audience, and the Colonel in the back room doing it to those with the bankrolls.

Surely, no one since Elvis has had a manager as conspicuous as Colonel Tom was in those early days. Does anyone even know who handles Sly Stallone or Bruce Springsteen? Does Sam Cohn, head of International Creative Management, walk up and down the aisle when his clients perform, chomping a cigar and renting Army surplus binoculars to fans for fifty cents a head? By modern standards of agenting, Colonel Tom was positively quaint.

But during the movie years, fans' perceptions of him shifted dramatically. He went from being a benevolent hustler to an evil manipulator. He took the blame for Elvis's abandoning the stage and getting trapped in all those movies like a dead fly in celluloid amber. It was the Colonel, after all, who always turned down interesting—i.e., risky—movie projects. And it was he who made the deal with Hill and Range Music Publishing Company that got Elvis all those insipid songs.

By 1968 even the Colonel was getting worried about the movies, which had sunk so low in exhibitors'

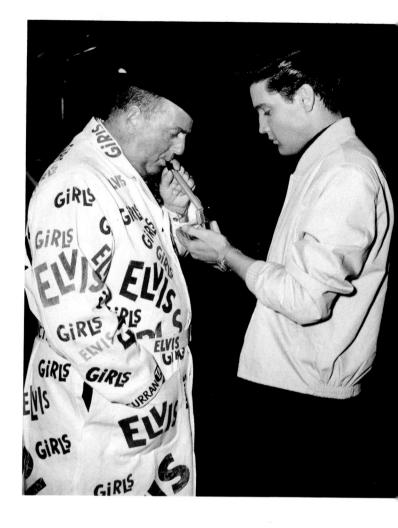

Could it be, as record producer Phil Spector contended, that Colonel Parker kept Elvis loyal through hypnosis? For those who see the movie years as a great promise unfulfilled, there is no satisfying explanation for why Elvis surrendered so much power to his manager, a former Hadacol salesman. But their partnership was unshakeable. When Elvis died, the Colonel announced, "This doesn't change a thing," and continued to merchandise his client until stopped by the courts.

Season's Greetings...
Elvis and the Colonel

The Colonel always portrayed Santa on the Christmas cards he and Elvis mailed each year. The card at left was from 1975. At right, for his TV special in December 1968, Elvis rejected the Colonel's joviality in favor of black-leather rock and roll.

eyes that they were playing on double bills with *Ghidra the Three-Headed Monster*. He decided it was time for Elvis to be seen once again on television, where he hadn't appeared since 1960—on "Frank Sinatra's Welcome Home Party for Elvis Presley."

But the Colonel's idea for a TV special was an hour of sanctimonious programming called "Elvis and the Wonderful World of Christmas." His boy would stand center-stage in a tuxedo, crooning carols, surrounded by pirouetting elves and Santas.

After a decade of Hollywood gelding, after too many movie lullabies sung to cute kiddie co-stars, Elvis had had enough. He was spurred to make his stand against the Colonel by producer Steve Binder, who hammered home the fleeting nature of fame by taking him on a walk down Sunset Boulevard—where not one passer-by recognized Elvis Presley. Elvis could not

afford to continue being bland. He vetoed Colonel Parker's concept.

And so for the "Singer Special," aired December 3, 1968, a star was reborn. This television show was no nostalgia trip, no exhumation of a vanished teen heartthrob. Elvis was all heat and sex, dressed neck to ankle in tight black leather, snarling at the camera, more dangerous than ever before in his career. He gave familiar material the gruff authority of his mature voice, and he reintroduced full-barrel rockers like "Trouble" and "Tiger Man" (the latter performed in the show's 1969 rerun). Some sequences were so steamy (like the one in which he sings "Let Yourself Go" to a bevy of orgiastically gyrating girls in flimsy harem pants) that they were censored out by NBC.

The movie years were emphatically over. Elvis was back, and he was headed for Las Vegas.

Elvis's Lyrics

Although Elvis never wrote a song, he was known by his lyrics. Blue suede shoes, hound dogs, teddy bears: all became icons of Elvis World because he sang about them.

These verses from his songs show how much his musical identity changed during his career—from the emotional fever of the 1950s, to the cheerful movie songs of the early 1960s, to the mature musical explorations of the late 1960s and early 1970s, to the patriotism and religiosity of the final years. These are the words as Elvis sung them—in some cases changed from the songwriter's original lyrics.

1956 HEARTBREAK HOTEL
Mae Boren Axton, Tommy Durden, Elvis Presley

. . . Bellhop's tears keep flowin', desk clerk's
　　dressed in black
They been so long on lonely street they
　　ain't never gonna come back, oh!
I get so lonely
I get so lonely
Get so lonely I could die.

1956 RIP IT UP
Robert A. Blackwell, John S. Marascalco

Well it's Saturday night
And I just got paid
Fool about my money don't try to save
My heart says go go, have a good time
'Cause it's Saturday night
And I feel fine.
　　I'm gonna rip it up
　　I'm gonna rock it up
　　I'm gonna shake it up
　　I'm gonna ball it up
　　I'm gonna rip it up
　　And ball tonight.

1962   SONG OF THE SHRIMP

Roy C. Bennett, Sid Tepper
from the movie *Girls! Girls ! Girls!*

I saw three shrimp in the water
Two were old and gray
I swam a little bit closer
And I heard the third one say:

> Goodbye, mama shrimp
> Papa, shake my hand
> Here come the shrimp boat
> For to take me Louisian'.

Showed his mama and papa
Shrimp newspaper he read
An invitation to all the shrimp
And this is what it said:
Free ride—New Orleans
Stay in grand hotel
Meet Creole gal who help you
Come out of your shell.

If I should live to be ninety
I will never forget
The little shrimp and the song he sang
As he jumped into the net.

Goodbye, mama shrimp . . . (repeat chorus)

1963   COTTON CANDY LAND

B. Roberts, R. Batchelor
from the movie *It Happened at the World's Fair*

The sandman's comin', yes he's comin'
To sprinkle you with sand
He'll say one-two-three
And you will be in Cotton Candy Land

The sandman's comin', yes he's comin'
Will take you by the hand
And you'll ride upon a big white swan
In Cotton Candy Land.

You and the swan will float upon
A cloud of pink ice cream
Where every star is a candy bar
And the moon is a marshmallow dream.

1963   NO ROOM TO RHUMBA

Fred Wise, Dick Manning
from the movie *Fun in Acapulco*

. . . There's no room to rhumba in a sports car
You can't move forward or back
There's no room to do what the bee tells
  you to
Without throwin' your spine out of whack.

When a little kiss I want to steal
I hit my head against the steering wheel
Now I know the way a pretzel feels
All I can do is shout: Hey, let me out!

1966   HOW GREAT THOU ART

Stuart K. Hine

O Lord my God! When I in awesome wonder
Consider all the worlds Thy hands have
  made,
I see the stars, I hear the rolling thunder,
Thy power throughout the universe
  displayed.

Then sings my soul, my Savior God to Thee:
How great Thou art! How great Thou art!
Then sings my soul, my Savior God to Thee:
How great Thou art! How great Thou art!

1969 IN THE GHETTO (THE VICIOUS CIRCLE)
Mac Davis

As the snow flies on a cold and grey
  Chicago mornin'
A poor little baby child is born in the ghetto
And his mama cries
'Cause if there's one thing that she don't
  need it's another little hungry mouth to feed
In the ghetto.
People don't you understand the child
  needs a helping hand or he'll grow up to
  be an angry young man some day.
Take a look at you and me; are we too blind
  to see?
Or do we simply turn our heads and look
  the other way?
Well, the world turns
And a hungry little boy with a runny nose
  plays in the street as the cold wind blows
In the ghetto.

And his hunger burns
So he starts to roam the streets at night and
  he learns how to steal and he learns how
  to fight
In the ghetto.
And then one night in desperation, a young
  man breaks away
He buys a gun, steals a car, tries to run, but
  he don't get far, and his mama cries
As a crowd gathers 'round an angry young
  man, face down in the street with a gun
  in his hand
In the ghetto
As her young man dies on a cold and grey
  Chicago mornin' another little baby child
  is born
In the ghetto
And his mama cries.

1972 AN AMERICAN TRILOGY
Mickey Newbury

Oh I wish I was in the land of cotton
Old things they are not forgotten
Look away, look away, look away Dixieland.
Oh I wish I was in Dixie, away, away
In Dixieland I take my stand to live and die
  in Dixie.
Cause, Dixieland, that's where I was born
Early, Lord, one frosty mornin'
Look away, look away, look away, Dixieland.

Glory, glory hallelujah
Glory, glory hallelujah
Glory, glory hallelujah
His truth is marching on.

So hush little baby
Don't you cry
You know your daddy's bound to die
But all my trials, Lord soon be over.

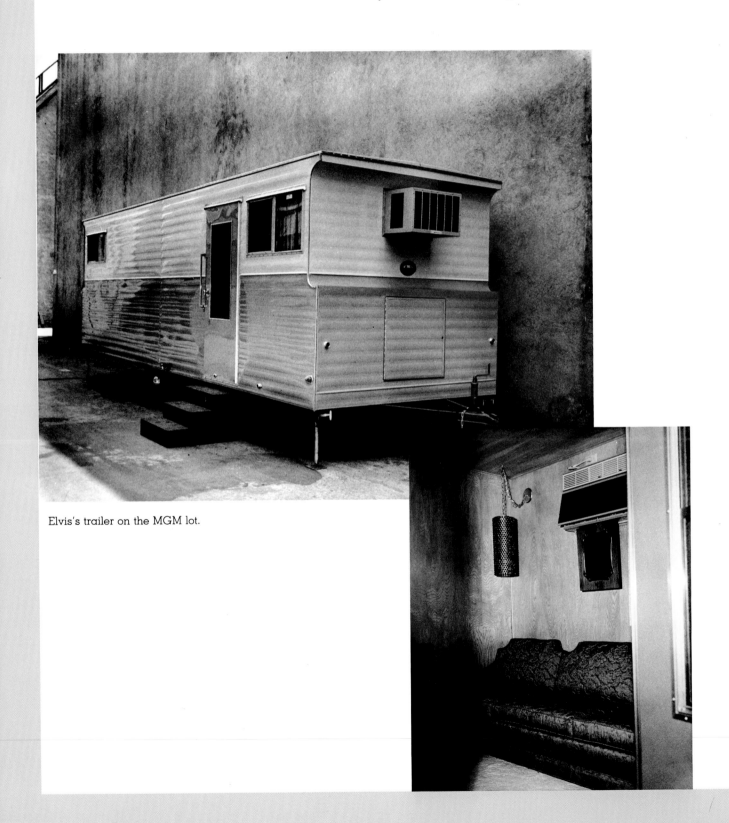

Elvis's trailer on the MGM lot.

LOVE ME TENDER

20th Century–Fox, 1956

Elvis as a southerner in trouble with the North: he is the youngest of four brothers pursued by Union troops after the Civil War. This is the only movie in which he dies on screen.

Elvis plays Clint Reno. Co-stars: Debra Paget, Richard Egan. Director: Robert D. Webb.

Songs: "Love Me Tender"; "Let Me Be"; "Poor Boy"; "We're Gonna Move."

LOVING YOU

Paramount, 1957

Art imitates life: Elvis plays a country boy who sings his way to fame and fortune.

Elvis plays "Deke Rivers" (stage name of Jimmy Thompkins). Co-stars: Lizabeth Scott, Dolores Hart, Wendell Corey. Director: Hal Kanter.

Songs: "Got a Lot o' Livin' to Do"; "Hot Dog"; "Lonesome Cowboy"; "Loving You"; "Mean Woman Blues"; "Party"; "Teddy Bear."

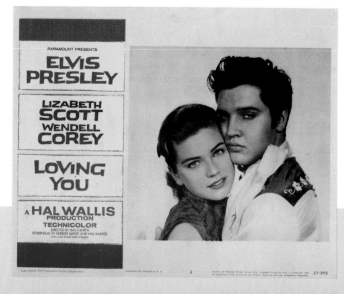

JAILHOUSE ROCK
MGM, 1957

As an ex-con with a chip on his shoulder, Elvis gains fame by singing but loses his soul because he is so greedy. A career-threatening accident (he gets socked in the vocal cords) brings him to his senses.

Elvis plays Vince Everett. Co-stars: Judy Tyler, Mickey Shaughnessy. Director: Richard Thorpe.

Songs: "Baby I Don't Care"; "Don't Leave Me Now"; "I Wanna Be Free"; "Jailhouse Rock"; "One More Day" (sung by Elvis's cellmate Hunk Houghton [Mickey Shaughnessy]); "Treat Me Nice"; "Young and Beautiful."

KING CREOLE
Paramount, 1958

Sauntering the mean streets of New Orleans, Elvis battles hoods, meets a hooker with a heart of gold, and winds up with a woman of virtue. Based on Harold Robbins's *A Stone for Danny Fisher*, originally acquired as a vehicle for James Dean.

Elvis plays Danny Fisher. Co-stars: Carolyn Jones, Dolores Hart, Lilliane Montevecchi, Dean Jagger, Walter Matthau. Director: Michael Curtiz.

Songs: "As Long As I Have You"; "Crawfish"; "Dixieland Rock"; "Don't Ask Me Why"; "Hard-Headed Woman"; "King Creole"; "Lover Doll"; "New Orleans"; "Steadfast, Loyal and True"; "Trouble"; "Turtles, Berries and Gumbo" (sung by street vendors); "Young Dreams."

Judy Tyler and Jennifer Holden dig the Presley beat on the set of *Jailhouse Rock*.

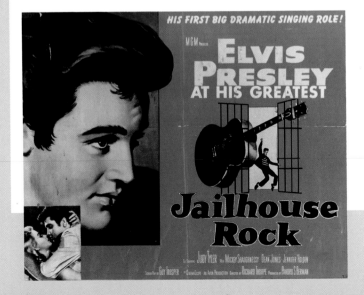

The outsider in *Flaming Star*, torn between Kiowa and white man's ways.

G.I. BLUES
Paramount, 1960

A salute to Elvis's Army years in Germany. He plays a khaki-clad lothario who bets his buddies he can bed the showgirl with the five-foot-long legs. He wins her by earnestly diapering a baby.

Elvis plays Tulsa McLean. Co-star: Juliet Prowse. Director: Norman Taurog.

Songs: "Big Boots"; "Blue Suede Shoes"; "Didja Ever"; "Doin' the Best I Can"; "Frankfurt Special"; "G.I. Blues"; "Pocketful of Rainbows"; "Shoppin' Around"; "Tonight Is So Right for Love"; "What's She Really Like"; "Wooden Heart."

FLAMING STAR
20th Century–Fox, 1960

In a role written for Marlon Brando, Elvis plays a half-breed in the middle of a small-town Texas race war. His most earnest acting job, and one of his few commercial flops.

Elvis plays Pacer Burton. Co-stars: Barbara Eden, Dolores Del Rio, Steve Forrest. Director: Don Siegel.

Songs: "A Cane and a High Starched Collar"; "Flaming Star."

WILD IN THE COUNTRY

20th Century–Fox, 1961

Clifford Odets's literate screenplay casts Elvis as a punk on probation who learns about civilized society from psychiatric social worker Hope Lange. She uncovers his writing talent. His short story is published and he heads off to college.

Elvis plays Glenn Tyler. Co-stars: Hope Lange, Tuesday Weld, Millie Perkins, Rafer Johnson, John Ireland. Director: Philip Dunne.

Songs: "In My Way"; "I Slipped, I Stumbled, I Fell"; "Lonely Man"; "Wild in the Country."

BLUE HAWAII

Paramount, 1961

Heir to a pineapple fortune, Elvis wants to prove he can make it on his own. He chooses a career as a tourist guide. After much parent-son strife, he reconciles with his family by agreeing to do all the travel arrangements for a convention of his father's pineapple employees. Elvis's biggest box-office success.

Elvis plays Chad Gates. Co-stars: Joan Blackman, Nancy Walters, Roland Winters, Angela Lansbury. Director: Norman Taurog.

Songs: "Almost Always True"; "Aloha Oe"; "Beach Boy Blues"; "Blue Hawaii"; "Can't Help Falling in Love"; "Hawaiian Sunset"; "Hawaiian Wedding Song"; "Island of Love"; "Ito Eats"; "Ku-U-I-Po"; "Moonlight Swim"; "No More"; "Rock-A-Hula Baby"; "Slicin' Sand".

FOLLOW THAT DREAM

United Artists, 1962

When their jalopy runs out of gas, Elvis and his wacky white-trash relatives decide to homestead in Florida. But a nearby craps game keeps them awake at night. Using judo, Elvis routs the gamblers, then does battle against the state welfare system that wants to take his adopted kin away.

Elvis plays Toby Kwimper. Co-stars: Anne Helm, Joanna Moore, Arthur O'Connell. Director: Gordon Douglas.

Songs: "Follow That Dream"; "I'm Not the Marrying Kind"; "Sound Advice"; "What a Wonderful Life."

KID GALAHAD

United Artists, 1962

As a guy with a great set of pipes, an iron jaw, and anvil hands, Elvis breezes unscathed through the violent and corrupt boxing underworld. He licks the bad guys, wins the big fight, and marries the girl.

Elvis plays Walter Gulick. Co-stars: Lola Albright, Joan Blackman, Gig Young, Charles Bronson. Director: Phil Karlson.

Songs: "A Whistling Tune"; "Home Is Where the Heart Is"; "I Got Lucky"; "King of the Whole Wide World"; "Riding the Rainbow"; "This Is Living."

Elvis celebrates his twenty-sixth birthday while filming *Wild in the Country.*

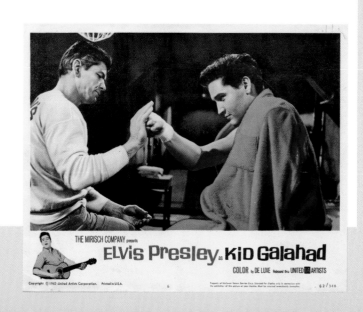

GIRLS! GIRLS! GIRLS!

Paramount, 1962

Elvis saves his charter fishing boat from a rich man who cares nothing about the sea. Sage Oriental advice is dispensed by Benson Fong.

Elvis plays Ross Carpenter. Co-stars: Stella Stevens, Laurel Goodwin, Jeremy Slate. Director: Norman Taurog.

Songs: "A Boy Like Me, A Girl Like You"; "Earth Boy"; "Girls! Girls! Girls!"; "I Don't Want to Be Tied"; "Return to Sender"; "Song of the Shrimp"; "Thanks to the Rolling Sea"; "The Walls Have Ears"; "We'll Be Together"; "We're Coming In Loaded"; "Where Do You Come From?"

IT HAPPENED AT THE WORLD'S FAIR

MGM, 1963

A pilot with no money and no plane, Elvis hangs out at the Seattle World's Fair, where he falls in love with the nurse at the first-aid station and feeds endless amounts of junk food to an orphaned Chinese tyke.

Elvis plays Mike Edwards. Co-stars: Joan O'Brien, Gary Lockwood, Vicky Tiu. Director: Norman Taurog.

Songs: "A World of Our Own"; "Beyond the Bend"; "Cotton Candy Land"; "Happy Ending"; "How Would You Like to Be"; "I'm Falling in Love Tonight"; "One Broken Heart for Sale"; "Relax"; "Take Me to the Fair"; "They Remind Me Too Much of You."

FUN IN ACAPULCO
Paramount, 1963

Elvis gets a job as a lifeguard at an Acapulco hotel and finds himself caught between an amorous lady bullfighter and the hotel's social director. He triumphs over acrophobia by jumping off the cliffs of La Quebrada into the raging sea.

Elvis plays Mike Windgren. Co-stars: Ursula Andress, Elsa Cardenas. Director: Richard Thorpe.

Songs: "Bossa Nova Baby"; "The Bullfighter Was a Lady"; "El Toro"; "Fun in Acapulco"; "Guadalajara"; "I Think I'm Gonna Like It Here"; "Marguerita"; "Mexico"; "There's No Room to Rhumba in a Sports Car"; "Vino, Dinero y Amor."

KISSIN' COUSINS
MGM, 1964

Elvis in two roles: a blond hillbilly and a black-haired Army officer. Dark Elvis must convince light Elvis that it's okay to build a nuclear missile silo near the family's moonshine still.

Elvis plays Josh Morgan and Jodie Tatum. Co-stars: Arthur O'Connell, Glenda Farrell, Jack Albertson, Pamela Austin, Cynthia Pepper, Yvonne Craig. Director: Gene Nelson.

Songs: "Barefoot Ballad"; "Catchin' On Fast"; "Kissin' Cousins"; "Once Is Enough"; "One Boy, Two Little Girls"; "Smokey Mountain Boy"; "Tender Feeling"; "There's Gold in the Mountains."

Elvis makes friends with a *Kissin' Cousins* co-star by giving a basket of dog valuables.

VIVA LAS VEGAS

MGM, 1964

Race car driver Elvis falls in love with hotel swimming instructor Ann-Margret. When his money (the entry fee for the "big race") gets sucked down the drain of the swimming pool, he takes a job as a waiter and competes with Ann-Margret in the employees' talent contest. He enters the race, wins, and marries A-M.

Elvis plays Lucky Jackson. Co-star: Ann-Margret. Director: George Sidney.

Songs: "C'mon Everybody"; "If You Think I Don't Need You"; "I Need Somebody to Lean On"; "The Lady Loves Me"; "Santa Lucia"; "Today, Tomorrow and Forever"; "Viva Las Vegas"; "What'd I Say"; "Yellow Rose of Texas."

ROUSTABOUT

Paramount, 1964

Elvis goes from singing shill in a fortune-teller's teahouse to carnival roustabout, where his musical talents keep the midway alive.

Elvis plays Charlie Rogers. Co-stars: Barbara Stanwyck, Joan Freeman, Leif Erickson, Sue Ane Langdon, Joan Staley. Director: John Rich.

Songs: "Big Love, Big Heartache"; "Carny Town"; "Hard Knocks"; "It's a Wonderful World"; "It's Carnival Time"; "Little Egypt"; "One Track Heart"; "Poison Ivy League"; "Roustabout"; "There's a Brand New Day on the Horizon"; "Wheels on My Heels."

ALLIED ARTISTS PICTURE CORPORATION PRESENTS

ELVIS PRESLEY

in

"TICKLE ME" (U)

Co-starring

JULIE ADAMS   JOCELYN LANE   JACK MULLANEY

PANAVISION®   DE LUXE COLOR®

RELEASED BY WARNER-PATHE DISTRIBUTORS LTD.

GIRL HAPPY

MGM, 1965

Elvis is hired as a chaperone for the nubile daughter of Big Frank, a Chicago nightclub owner with underworld connections. The girl gets drunk in Fort Lauderdale, does a striptease in public, and winds up in jail. Big Frank is angry, but forgives Elvis when he realizes that Elvis means well.

Elvis plays Rusty Wells. Co-stars: Shelley Fabares, Gary Crosby, Harold J. Stone, Toby Baker, Nita Talbot, Mary Ann Mobley. Director: Boris Sagal.

Song: "Cross My Heart and Hope to Die"; "Do Not Disturb"; "Do the Clam"; "Fort Lauderdale Chamber of Commerce"; "Girl Happy"; "I've Got to Find My Baby"; "The Meanest Girl in Town"; "Puppet on a String"; "Spring Fever"; "Startin' Tonight"; "Wolf Call."

TICKLE ME

Allied Artists, 1965

Elvis as an out-of-work rodeo cowboy at an all-girl beauty spa. He escapes a dozen man-hungry women in jogging suits, falls for the physical instructor, and stumbles upon a jillion dollars' worth of hidden gold.

Elvis plays Lonnie Beale. Co-stars: Jocelyn Lane, Julie Adams, Jack Mullaney, Merry Anders, Connie Gilchrist. Director: Norman Taurog.

Songs: "Dirty, Dirty Feeling"; "Easy Question"; "I Feel That I've Known You Forever"; "I'm Yours"; "Night Rider"; "Put the Blame on Me"; "Slowly but Surely."

"GIRL HAPPY"
A Metro-Goldwyn-Mayer Release

.....*It's* **Fun!**
.....*It's* **Girls!**
.....*It's* **Song!**
.....*It's* **Color!**
It's
ELVIS!

ELVIS PRESLEY
"TICKLE ME"

See ELVIS take on the rodeo...the robbers...and the Ghost House!

HARUM SCARUM

MGM, 1965

Decked out in caftan and turban, Elvis is a movie star publicizing his new film, who gets kidnapped by evildoers, meets beautiful Princess Shalimar, and karate-chops his way out of the Arab world.

Elvis plays Johnny Tyronne. Co-stars: Mary Ann Mobley, Fran Jeffries, Michael Ansara. Director: Gene Nelson.

Songs: ''Go East, Young Man''; ''Golden Coins''; ''Harem Holiday''; ''Hey Little Girl''; ''Kismet''; ''Mirage''; ''My Desert Serenade''; ''Shake That Tambourine''; ''So Close Yet So Far.''

FRANKIE AND JOHNNY

United Artists, 1966

When Frankie (Donna Douglas) shoots Johnny (Elvis) because she is jealous of Nellie Bly (Nancy Kovack), he is saved by his lucky cricket pendant.

Elvis plays Johnny. Co-stars: Donna Douglas, Nancy Kovack, Sue Ane Langdon. Director: Fred de Cordova.

Songs: ''Beginner's Luck''; ''Chesay''; ''Come Along''; ''Down by the Riverside''; ''When the Saints Go Marching In''; ''Everybody Come Aboard''; ''Frankie and Johnny''; ''Hard Luck''; ''Look Out, Broadway''; ''Petunia, the Gardener's Daughter''; ''Please Don't Stop Loving Me''; ''Shout It Out''; ''What Every Woman Lives For.''

Elvis eagerly made *Harum Scarum* because it fulfilled his boyhood fantasy of being Valentino.

PARADISE, HAWAIIAN STYLE

Paramount, 1966

Fired as an airlines pilot for kissing a stewardess, Elvis returns to his native Hawaii and starts a helicopter taxi service. While ferrying a chopper full of unruly show dogs, he accidentally buzzes an auto on the highway—which turns out to be driven by an inspector from the Federal Aviation Agency. He saves his skin by performing a heroic rescue.

Elvis plays Rick Richards. Co-stars: Suzanna Leigh, James Shigeta, Donna Butterworth, Marianna Hill, Irene Tsu, Linda Wong. Director: Michael Moore.

Songs: "Datin'"; "Dog's Life"; "Drums of the Islands"; "House of Sand"; "Paradise Hawaiian Style"; "Queenie Wahine's Papaya"; "Scratch My Back"; "Stop Where You Are"; "This Is My Heaven."

SPINOUT

MGM, 1966

Elvis is pursued by a millionaire's daughter, a drummer, and a feminist author researching a book called *The Perfect Male*.

Elvis plays Mike McCoy. Co-stars: Shelley Fabares, Diane McBain, Deborah Walley, Dodie Marshall. Director: Norman Taurog.

Songs: "Adam and Evil"; "All That I Am"; "Am I Ready?"; "Beach Shack"; "I'll Be Back"; "Never Say Yes"; "Smorgasbord"; "Stop, Look and Listen"; "Spinout."

Elvis has a tough time deciding which of the three beautiful brides-to-be (Diane McBain, Deborah Walley and Shelley Fabares) will be his own.

EASY COME, EASY GO

Paramount, 1967

Elvis the frogman demolition expert in search of buried treasure. On land, he encounters a kooky yoga instructor, beatnik body painters, and the most surreal go-go club since "The Purple Pit" in Jerry Lewis's *The Nutty Professor*.

Elvis plays Ted Jackson. Co-stars: Dodie Marshall, Pat Priest, Pat Harrington. Director: John Rich.

Songs: "Easy Come, Easy Go"; "I'll Take Love"; "The Love Machine"; "Sing, You Children"; "Yoga Is as Yoga Does"; "You Gotta Stop."

DOUBLE TROUBLE

MGM, 1967

Mod adventures in Beatles country: Elvis is pursued across the continent by sexy girls in miniskirts, the bumbling Wiere Brothers, smugglers, and angry Uncle Gerald.

Elvis plays Guy Lambert. Co-stars: Annette Day, John Williams, Yvonne Romain, the Wiere Brothers. Director: Norman Taurog.

Songs: "Baby If You'll Give Me All of Your Love"; "City by Night"; "Could I Fall in Love"; "Double Trouble"; "I Love Only One Girl"; "Long-Legged Girl"; "Old MacDonald"; "There Is So Much World to See."

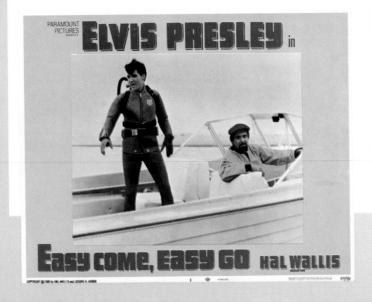

CLAMBAKE

United Artists, 1967

Elvis (a rich guy) trades identities with a poor guy so that people will like him for himself instead of his money. A gold-digger girl who wants to fall in love with a rich guy falls for Elvis, much to her dismay, but then gets happy when he reveals he owns half the planet.

Elvis plays Scott Heyward. Co-stars: Shelley Fabares, Will Hutchins, Bill Bixby, Gary Merrill, James Gregory. Director: Arthur Nadel.

Songs: "Clambake"; "Confidence"; "The Girl I Never Loved"; "Hey, Hey, Hey"; "A House That Has Everything"; "Who Needs Money"; "You Don't Know Me."

STAY AWAY, JOE

MGM, 1968

Elvis is an Indian: brown-skinned, hot-blooded, and hard-drinking. Elvis sings to Dominick the Bull, a family pet who gets eaten by drunken Indians who mistake him for a cow.

Elvis plays Joe Lightcloud. Co-stars: Burgess Meredith, Joan Blondell, Katy Jurado, Thomas Gomez. Director: Peter Tewksbury.

Songs: "All I Needed Was the Rain"; "Dominick"; "Stay Away, Joe."

Elvis is befuddled by the antics of the counter-culture in *Easy Come, Easy Go*.

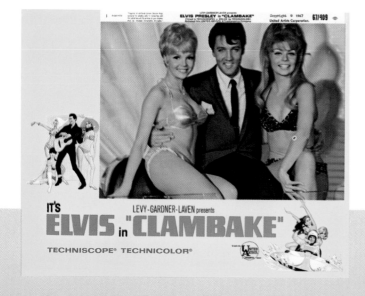

SPEEDWAY

MGM, 1968

Race car driver Elvis is investigated by white-booted IRS agent Nancy Sinatra. He sings about how good it is to pay taxes to Uncle Sam, wins enough money in the big race to get the government off his back, and winds up in a wild disco fantasy with Nancy.

Elvis plays Steve Grayson. Co-stars: Nancy Sinatra, Bill Bixby, Gale Gordon. Director: Norman Taurog.

Songs: "He's Your Uncle, Not Your Dad"; "Let Yourself Go"; "Speedway"; "There Ain't Nothin' Like a Song"; "Who Are You"; "Your Groovy Self (Nancy Sinatra)"; "Your Time Hasn't Come Yet, Baby."

LIVE A LITTLE, LOVE A LITTLE

MGM, 1968

Fashion photographer Elvis (a responsible adult for a change) is pursued by a man-hungry woman and her Great Dane. The pressure is so heavy that he has a surrealistic dream in which his dance partner wears a dog suit.

Elvis plays Greg. Co-stars: Michele Carey, Rudy Vallee, Don Porter, Dick Sargent, Sterling Holloway. Director: Norman Taurog.

Songs: "A Little Less Conversation"; "Almost in Love"; "Edge of Reality"; "Wonderful World."

Hounded by the Internal Revenue Service, Elvis sings about fiscal responsibility in *Speedway*.

Elvis, Nancy and Bill Bixby set things swinging at the racing club discotheque.

MGM presents "**SPEEDWAY**" PANAVISION® and METROCOLOR

Elvis lets loose with a swinging song and dance during a wild dream sequence.

MGM presents A Douglas Laurence Production "**LIVE A LITTLE, LOVE A LITTLE**" In PANAVISION® And METROCOLOR

CHARRO!
National General, 1969

An *hommage* to Clint Eastwood westerns, with stubble-faced Elvis squinting and wearing a dirty serape, and singing nothing more than the title song. A major departure from the happy-go-lucky mold.

Elvis plays Jesse Wade. Co-stars: Ina Balin, Victor French, Barbara Werle. Director: Charles Marquis Warren.

Song: "Charro."

THE TROUBLE WITH GIRLS
(AND HOW TO GET INTO IT)
MGM, 1969

Murder, kidnapping, union problems, and lynch-mob mentality are just some of the rollicking distractions Elvis faces as the leader of a troupe of traveling entertainers in the Roaring Twenties.

Elvis plays Walter Hale. Co-stars: Marilyn Mason, Nicole Jaffe, Sheree North, John Carradine. Director: Peter Tewksbury.

Songs: "Almost"; "Clean Up Your Own Backyard"; "Signs of the Zodiac"; "Swing Low, Sweet Chariot."

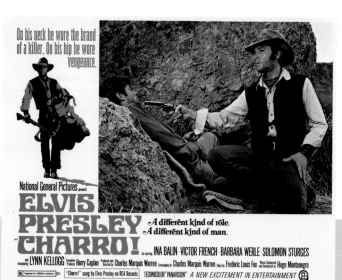

Elvis and Marilyn Mason spoof the "Bonnie and Clyde" characters.

CHANGE OF HABIT

NBC–Universal, 1969

Elvis the ghetto doctor teams up with three plain-clothes nuns to deal with slum housing, race relations, autism, and street crime. Because he doesn't know she is a nun, Elvis falls for Sister Michelle (Mary Tyler Moore) but can't figure out why she avoids him. The enigmatic ending doesn't reveal whether they consummate their relationship. Many glimmers of "the real Elvis" can be seen in the picture. Dr. Carpenter enjoys touch football, has a musical jam session with his friends, and wears a college sweatshirt indicating allegiance to Memphis, Tennessee.

Elvis plays Dr. John Carpenter. Co-stars: Mary Tyler Moore, Barbara McNair, Jane Elliot. Director: William Graham.

Songs: "Change of Habit"; "Have a Happy"; "Let Us Pray"; "Rubberneckin'."

Documentary Films

ELVIS: THAT'S THE WAY IT IS

MGM, 1970

ELVIS ON TOUR

MGM, 1972

THIS IS ELVIS

MGM, 1981

A posthumous semidocumentary biography that intercuts real footage with reenacted scenes in which actors play Elvis.

"A Presley picture is the only sure thing in show business."
—Producer Hal Wallis

Gilded Elvis

Now that the 1950s have receded safely into the realm of nostalgia, it is easy to appreciate the allure of early Elvis: Elvis the young rebel in his baggy jacket. Pure Elvis. Primitive Elvis. Elvis singing out the battle cry of rock and roll.

But what about Elvis of the 1970s? This is no mere rock-and-roll singer. This is gilded Elvis, a traveling coronation ceremony, a living legend, the King.

He is the Elvis whose garniture inspires impersonators and parodists. Elvis of the jewel-encrusted jumpsuit with tire-chain belt and elephantine bell-bottoms, Elvis of the jet-black blow-dry helmet hair and muttonchop sideburns. His eyeglasses look like mod construction girders, he wears diamonds as bright as Liberace's, and from the chains on his neck swing great gold crosses and a Hebrew *chai*, and mysterious totems with obscure meanings known only to his inner circle.

His voice is no longer the throaty whine of a hopeful young blues shouter. He is a bombastic basso buffo, lofting through two and one-third octaves, orating patriotic arias, religious hymns, and "My Way."

And he is more popular than ever. When he returned to the stage in Las Vegas in July 1969, his fans, deprived of their man for nearly a decade, packed the largest venue in town, twice a night, for a month. And for the next eight years, two engagements per year in Las Vegas and 1,126 shows in the biggest auditoriums America's cities and towns had to offer, Elvis never played to an empty seat.

His movie career, with the exception of documentaries, was over. Everything Elvis had, he gave to his concerts. The stage—where he had first electrified the country in the 1950s—once again became his medium.

Elvis concerts of the 1950s had offered music as sexual release. In the 1970s, sheer sexuality was transcended for a more spiritual experience.

There was the real possibility that something big might happen, that Elvis might—as he did in Asheville, North Carolina, in 1975—call up people from the crowd to give them diamond rings or his guitar. Or that he would fling his jeweled cape to the multitudes, or reach down from the stage and offer his touch, or throw out a sweat-stained scarf, or point a finger, and merely by singling someone out, lift their burdens.

It didn't matter if you came away empty-handed. To the faithful, being in his presence was enough. "It was as if he were a momentary gift," writes Samuel Roy in *Elvis, Prophet of Power*, "too special to be real, too precious to be deserved, too illuminating to last."

He was Monty Hall and Jesus rolled into one, a perfect master to his idolaters. And when critics complained that his singing wasn't up to snuff or he was overweight or his outfits were tacky, well, they just didn't understand that it was ELVIS they were looking at, not just some guy singing a song.

One did not attend an Elvis concert to hear new songs or see new things. One went as one goes to hear a favorite symphony or see a classic film. The point is to bask in it, to know that for as long as it lasts, all will be well with the world.

He had flopped when he played Las Vegas in 1956. In 1969 he returned to conquer, shattering attendance records.

An Elvis concert was a ceremonial event, repeated with minor variations. If Elvis was in good voice, or if he looked slim, or if he joked with the audience, so much the better. But even if he mumbled, split his pants, and looked ill, he was still Elvis—and that is what the people came for.

The pageantry begins with the heraldic horns and drumbeat of *Also sprach Zarathustra*, the theme from *2001*. From that moment to the inevitable final words, "Elvis has left the building," audiences are rapt by the preordained—but always wondrous—enthronement of Elvis.

Even the music itself takes on a ritual form, as listeners eagerly await, then cheer, each song's great moment: the soaring "Oh MY GOD, how great thou art" in "How Great Thou Art," the electrifying tempo change in "Suspicious Minds," the hollering "Glory, glory, hallelujah" climax to "American Trilogy." Backing Elvis are J. D. Sumner (with the Stamps), a basso profundo who rumbles auditoriums more than Sensurround, and

at the other extreme, Kathy Westmoreland, a coloratura soprano who can hit high notes only angels hear. And there are trumpets and trombones, guitars, drums, and a lonely flute. It is the musical macrocosm, all voices behind one, a portrait of Elvis as master of the musical universe.

The new Elvis incorporates the crotch thrusts of Tom Jones with tai chi arabesques. Martial arts are an Elvis passion; the mummery of karate now infuses his legendary stage movement. No longer the lurchin' urchin, he is an eighth-degree black belt; now formal gestures are part of the protocol. *Variety*'s review of his Las Vegas show in 1970 calls it "the essence of Kabuki drama." *Every* move is known and treasured by the faithful: the licked lip, the upraised eyes, the bowed head.

He commandeers the stage like a general leading a charge, whipping his cape, snapping the mike cord,

One and a half billion people watched "Elvis— Aloha from Hawaii" broadcast by satellite in 1973.

Above: Photo taken at Nassau Coliseum, New York, by Elvis fan Kathy Curlis on July 19, 1975. After Elvis died, she and her friend Donna Gaffin sent the picture to Vernon Presley with this inscription: "Just a small thank you for giving us your 'son.' He was the 'Sunshine of our lives.' Love and peace thru Elvis."

thrusting forward as if a bayonet were fixed on the end of his guitar. But even better than his moving is the way he poses, still as a statue, creating moments of perfect Elvisness. Each is a grandiloquent rendering of heroic struggle, or yearning, or humility, or an attitude that is pure, abstract, indescribable Elvis—legs bowed in a slight crouch, head aimed forward, both hands pointing to the side like parallel pistols. Grab the Instamatic and shoot! Even as a tiny blur captured from the back row, each pose is unmistakably Elvis.

More than any other part of the show, the embellishment that has come to symbolize Elvis of the 1970s is his jumpsuit. What a strange piece of clothing!

The gaudiest jumpsuits are unbelievably cumbersome raiments, comparable only to a coronation robe. Some weigh as much as thirty pounds. The belt, with its buckle, chains, and studs, can add another ten. Simply holding an Elvis jumpsuit in one's hands for any length of time is exhausting. To wear it, and move and sing under hot lights, is a feat. And yet, for gilded Elvis to wear ordinary, comfortable clothes onstage would be wrong. The weight is a burden of his office.

His 1950s stagewear had been street duds that suggested a rebellious attitude towards fashion. The jumpsuits, however, are far removed from functional clothing. Although they feature fashion cues of their time, such as bellbottoms, rhinestones, and extra-wide belts, they go beyond fashion to pure symbolism.

He began wearing them the same year astronauts walked the moon in their own silver jumpsuits. In addition to out-of-this-world heroes, the other exponents of the jumpsuit are garage mechanics, for whom it is a modern-day version of overalls. How perfectly Elvoid: way out, but down-and-dirty.

A belt four inches wide with a gold buckle nearly as big as a dinner tray makes the outfit that of a champion. Such belts belong to gladiators who have licked all the competition. The wearer is a conqueror, the top of the heap, a mean dude. The belt and buckle attest to the fact that Elvis *won* his crown. In fact, Elvis *did* earn the gold belt in 1969 for "the world's championship attendance record" at the Las Vegas International Hotel, later renamed the Hilton.

The high collar and cape signify old-fashioned gallantry. Superheroes wear capes; so did Confederate officers. The whoosh of a cape around the shoulders might also suggest the irresistible (but dangerous) magnetism of a vampire. Think about it: Dracula in a car coat or Superman in a poncho wouldn't be nearly so impressive.

Beyond all their cultural associations, Elvis's suits are emblazoned with specific symbols of power, wealth, and ferocity. Fans name them accordingly: the Prehistoric Bird, the Mexican Sundial, the King of Spades, the Inca Gold Leaf, the Black Eagle, the Mad Tiger.

When Specialists Elvis, a Japanese fan club, published a complete account of every concert Elvis gave between 1970 and 1977, all 1,126 performances were detailed by their attendance figures, location, time and date, and—most important—by which jumpsuit Elvis wore, its color and nickname, plus a full account of the belt, buckle, and scarf that went with it.

Photo taken at the Cow Palace, San Francisco, by Sheila Flaherty on November 13, 1970. "I could see every move, hear every word, and at times felt that I was right at his feet and he was singing to only me."

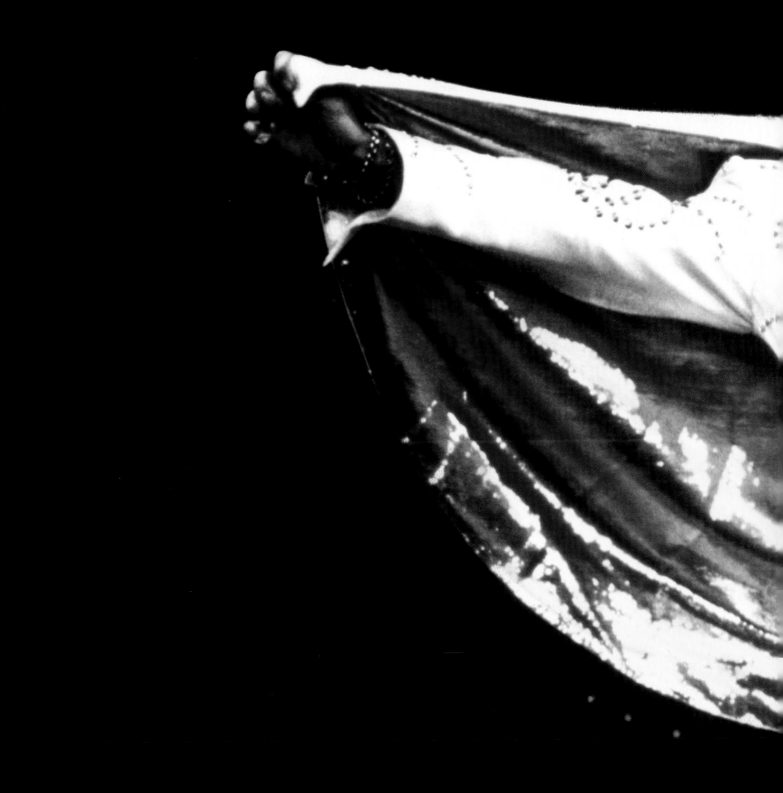

Elvis didn't like being called King, but it was inevitable. That he became a King rather than a Chairman of the Board, like Sinatra, or a Boss like Springsteen, was a matter of geographical destiny. The South loves royalty, from the pomp of the Mardi Gras to Memphis's yearly King Cotton Ball. Flip through southern school yearbooks, even in these egalitarian times, and you will see prom queens and homecoming kings galore. Many small towns are ruled for a day by their Watermelon Queen or Frog Jump Queen. And if nobody appoints him, a good ol' boy just might crown himself. Back roads of the rural South are a pageant of Upholstery Kings, Catfish Kings, and Barbecue Kings.

Elvis of the 1970s—once the King of Rock and Roll—graduated to being simply the King, no modifiers needed.

Only kings act the way Elvis did—absolutely certain of their position, no need to be uppity or to prove anything. That's why the people loved him: he spent lots of money, and when the bankroll got low, he made some more. He didn't care about any of the puzzling things that social climbers care about, like joining a secret society at Yale, marrying into the "right" family, and making sure that even though you are as rich as a pig, you appear shabby and understated.

He never invested a dime, and he paid more income tax than any other individual American in history. By the values of King Elvis, only a twit would be happy with some dreary tax shelter or paper stock certificate, when the same money could buy a custom-made twenty-four-karat-gold-trimmed Stutz Blackhawk.

Above: The King of Rock and Roll meets the Cotton King and Queen in Memphis, 1956. Right: Elvis accepts delivery of a new coach—his third Stutz Blackhawk. Far right: More generous than Santa Claus, he bought his maid a house and his nurse a mink coat, and gave away one hundred Cadillacs.

The TCB Oath

Written by Elvis in 1971 on a plane trip from Los Angeles to Memphis. (TCB means "Taking Care of Business," his personal paean to instant gratification.)

More self-respect, more respect for fellow man.
Respect for fellow students and instructors.
Respect for all styles and techniques.
Body conditioning, mental conditioning, meditation for calming and stilling of the mind and body.
Sharpen your skills, increase mental awareness for all those who might choose a new outlook and personal philosophy.
Freedom from constipation.

TCB TECHNIQUE
All techniques into one
Elvis Presley, 8th

Applying all techniques into one.

(Elvis writing "8th" did not mean that he fancied any resemblance between himself and King Henry VIII. It refers to his eighth-degree black belt.)

When the urge to give struck, he was never limited by middle-class notions of propriety. No etiquette of false humility held him back. And no tiresome cliché of "It's the thought that counts" ever clouded the royal joy he experienced from the colossal monetary value of the "happies" (his name for gifts) he gave. He even bestowed a ten-thousand-dollar jeweled robe upon Muhammad Ali and a thirty-thousand-dollar ring upon Sammy Davis, Jr. "Nobody thinks of giving a rich man anything," he explained.

He had it, and he flaunted it. He never lost the poor person's perspective of just how great money can be. And that is what made him the people's King. As eccentric as his spending was, even his most profligate behavior was all right, because the one thing he never became was a snob.

When he was declared King of Rock and Roll in 1956 and hit by an avalanche of adoration, survival demanded that he surround himself with guards to protect him from the awesome veneration of his subjects. First he pressed cousins and former high-school classmates into service. As his dominion broadened, the entourage flourished and expanded, drawn from Elvis's family, from his Army platoon, and from petitioners who weaseled through security.

King Elvis was never without his band of merry men. Some lived with him at Graceland, in the house or in trailers out back, or at the HoJo's down the road; when he was drafted, they accompanied him to basic training, then to Germany; they played bit parts in his movies. They became known as the Memphis Mafia.

By the 1970s, when Elvis took himself on tour, the palace guard had grown to magisterial proportions. The retinue included bodyguards and lackeys, a physician, a karate instructor, a hairdresser/spiritual advisor, his father, his cousins, his stepbrothers, his girlfriend, a jeweler ever ready with a case of diamond trinkets if the urge to buy should strike, the crew of his personal four-engine jet plane, sound and lighting men, his orchestra, backup singers, and concessionaires with official Elvis souvenirs. The entourage even had an officer to function as liaison with the business world—Colonel Parker, who had his own staff and chain of command.

Members of the court were bound together by a coat of arms created by Elvis: TCB with a lightning bolt,

Until he bought his own commercial-size airplane in 1975, Elvis was scared of flying. Named for his daughter, the four-engine *Lisa Marie* became his Graceland-away-from-home whenever he left to go on tour.

signifying "Taking Care of Business in a Flash." The heraldic insignia was emblazoned on an 11.5-karat diamond ring, spotlighted on the tail of his 880 Convair jet, the *Lisa Marie,* on badges and pendants worn by the inner circle. When asked to explain it, Elvis answered, "Quickness is what I dig."

The EP escutcheon also showed religious bearings. Elvis wore a Hebrew *chai* around his neck to signify solidarity with the chosen people. He wore a crucifix as well, joking, "Why miss heaven on a technicality?" (While making *Harum Scarum,* Elvis gave custom-made watches to every member of the cast and crew. The watches lit up every thirty seconds, alternating between a cross and a star of David.) He also wore a "tree of life" necklace, designed by Memphis Mafia foreman Marty Lacker and given to him by his faithful men—its branches inscribed with all the inner circle's names in Hebrew, Latin, and English, and with Elvis's name on the trunk.

Offstage, Elvis's favorite symbols of authority were not symbolic at all. He carried real badges that authorized him to arrest wrongdoers in both Memphis and Beverly Hills. He toted heavy-duty police-issue flashlights. And he almost always packed a gun.

His gun collection was not some outmoded array of showpiece weapons that an English lord might display in his smoking room. The ordnance was that of a red-blooded American male—guns that give power to the man who holds them; proper sword and scepter for a New World monarch. He liked nasty handguns especially: his "Dirty Harry" .44 magnum, a Derringer of the type favored by riverboat gamblers, a gold-inlaid Python, a turquoise-handled Colt .45. His favorite long guns were assault rifles and semiautomatics—weapons made for battle. Elvis had no interest in killing animals; he never shot anything except paper targets, televisions, and chandeliers.

His meeting with Richard Nixon took place because Elvis wanted a federal marshal's badge in order to carry his handguns across state lines. (He was, at the time, planning a one-man war against drug dealers.) As a professional courtesy—President to King—the wish was granted.

When Elvis was offered a deputy's badge by the Shelby County sheriff in Memphis, he insisted on a real sheriff's badge, with all the powers that came with it. The sheriff balked. Elvis threatened to run against him in the next election. Elvis got his badge.

When Elvis chose his queen, she was fourteen years old. He was twenty-five, far from the gilded personage that would evolve in the 1970s. But even in 1960, when Priscilla Beaulieu was selected for her beauty and her innocence, Elvis's urge for embellishment molded their relationship.

The stepdaughter of an Air Force officer stationed in Germany, Priscilla was discovered by one of Elvis's men and brought to a party at his off-base home in Bad Nauheim. After Elvis was discharged, he imported her to live at Graceland, to complete her education, and to be transformed into a suitable mate.

Under his tutelage, her crystalline blue eyes were lined with black eyeliner and weighted with false lashes. Lips were paled, skin was pancaked. Natural honey-brown hair was dyed with the exact shade of Clairol dye that Elvis used (Black Velvet). Then it was

Peter Noone (of Herman's Hermits) once fished for compliments by asking Elvis who was his favorite group. He replied, "The Los Angeles Police Department." He wasn't kidding. Elvis maintained a lifelong infatuation with law enforcement. Far left: President Nixon endorses Elvis's war on drugs; in uniform with Denver lawmen. Above: With Mississippi State Troopers in Tupelo. Left: The entourage—all newly deputized: Elvis totes a pearl-handled undercover .38; kneeling to his right is his personal physician, Dr. George Nichopolous; to his left is bodyguard Red West.

Below, center: Priscilla, 14 and unadorned, meets Elvis in Germany. Three years later, she attained peak Presley style.

mounded atop her head in a beehive that would have made Louis XIV's hairdresser jealous.

It was the style of the early 1960s, but infinitely more so. She looked like a queen, like Cleopatra of Egypt or the Ronettes of Phillies Records. By today's standards of beauty—even by the look of ordinary women in 1963—it is shocking. But could the ultimate American male marry someone who was not herself formulated as an extreme? Priscilla was a female projection of Elvis; and just as he manipulated the world so that all he wanted became his, and everything around him reflected his own style, so she became a mirror image of her creator.

She had no room to develop her own look and style. She couldn't even eat her favorite food—tuna salad—because Elvis didn't like the way it smelled. From a feminist point of view, her life was a horror. Look at pictures of seventeen-year-old Priscilla and you see a rather sad little girl underneath a towering hairdo. But step back and consider her through the eyes of the man who tried to forge her with the same audacity he had used to forge himself. Priscilla was a work of art, designed to be Elvis's own Adam's rib, the yin to his yang.

Of course, it is a silly notion; you cannot play with people like that, you cannot swallow a whole other identity in your craving to consume the world. But there is something poignant about those outlandish pictures of Priscilla in all her 1960s glory. She and Elvis were trying hard to make the symmetry between them work. She loved him. He loved her. Their hair was proof, high-rise evidence of the strongest kind of all-consuming passion.

Lisa Marie

Born February 1, 1968, exactly nine months after her mother and father were married, Lisa Marie Presley is Elvis's only child and sole heir to his estate.

To the King, she was a princess, and he spoiled her accordingly. She wore a child-size, full-length mink coat and a smiley face ring with diamonds for eyes, and drove around the lawn on her own custom-chromed golf cart.

Even after Elvis and Priscilla's divorce in 1973, Lisa Marie remained close to Elvis, often coming back to her gold-and-white fur-accented bedroom at Graceland. She was visiting on August 16, 1977, when Elvis died.

She has now grown up, but in Elvis World, Lisa Marie will always be her father's baby girl.

By the nature of their status above ordinary men, kings inspire tales of grandeur. People relish their immensity. Lore and legend sing of their superhuman qualities—their strength, their angelic goodness or consummate evil, their amazing abilities to outperform all others.

Elvis, for instance, if you believe what you read, ate more food than any other man who ever lived.

Take bacon. Elvis liked bacon, burnt to a crisp. Four pounds at a time, in a bowl for snacking, on top of the piano, accompanied by two large pizzas with the works. He liked cheeseburgers and could down a dozen at a time, topping off the meal with a gallon of ice cream. His dressing room at Paramount needed two refrigerator-freezers, one stocked exclusively with ice cream. He easily ingested fifteen tacos at a single sitting. He put so much pepper on his eggs they turned black and ate so many Spanish omelets that he created an egg shortage in Tennessee. Thirty cups of yogurt, eight massive honeydew melons, a hundred dollars' worth of ice cream bars: all gone in a night's eating binge. When he was on a diet, he confined himself to sausage biscuits, six or seven of them at a shot, sopped in a half pound of melted butter.

All of the above statistics are given as fact by Elvis's biographers. No doubt, the man had a healthy appetite; he always did; and in the final years, his metabolism slowed and trapped him. But what's wonderful about the preposterous accounts of his binges is that in the telling they become an everyday Elvis feat. If Elvis ever did anything once—and if anyone saw him do it—it was then written (in its most lurid and exaggerated form) part of the superhuman Elvis Legend.

When it came to Cadillacs, his appetite truly was superhuman. He was the Cadillac of Cadillac buyers, purchasing at least a hundred during his life. The most famous is the pink Fleetwood sedan he gave his mother in 1956. It didn't matter that she didn't drive. What was important was that the car sat glittering in the driveway for all to see and admire—a two-ton love trinket.

He arrived for his first screen test in two Cadillacs—one for him, one for his guitar.

Although he flirted with foreign oddities like a three-wheel Messerschmidt early in his buying career, then later grew fond of his six-door Mercedes limo and a couple of Rolls-Royces, Elvis never looked more correct than he did behind the wheel of a boat-size Caddy. The man and the car are the two best-known symbols of success America has ever produced.

He never bought less than the best and the most. His 1960 Cadillac limousine had a motorized shoeshine kit, a complete wet bar, a television, and a forty-five record player. His motorcycles had chrome, fringe, and candy-apple paint. When he decided he enjoyed slot-car racing, he added an entire room to Graceland for the track.

Elvis's staggering generosity was the stuff of which legends are made. Educated guessers estimate he gave away a million dollars' worth of diamonds. He gave away homes, cars, mink coats, trips to Hawaii, thousand-dollar bills, gift certificates to McDonald's, his own shirts, shoes, and prescription glasses. Nearly everyone who worked for Elvis got at least a car; but even total strangers—in the right place when the whim struck—became Elvis almsmen.

He gave a wheelchair (motorized, natch) to an old black lady he read about in the newspaper. He gave five hundred dollars to a blind man selling pencils on the streets of Memphis—and didn't even take a pencil! At Christmas (his favorite holiday), he and his father went downtown with a hundred thousand-dollar checks for Memphis charities. He bought the presidential yacht *Potomac*, then gave it to Danny Thomas for St. Jude Children's Research Hospital. He gave fifty thousand dollars to the motion picture relief fund, five thousand to the Jerry Lewis Muscular Dystrophy Telethon, and crisp hundred-dollar bills to cook Mary Jenkins when he was overwhelmed with gratitude after eating her macaroni salad.

One time Elvis made a midnight run to the dealer to buy Eldorados for two of his deserving guys. He noticed a young man and woman peering in the window. They looked needy. Elvis told them to pick the car of their choice, wrote out the check, and left them with the salesman to figure out the paperwork.

Then there was the time Colorado newscaster Don Kinney read an item on the air about Elvis giving away seven assorted Cadillacs and Lincolns to some locals. He joked, "Mr. Presley, I would not like to have a Cadillac—I'd rather have a little sports car." A Seville—as close as Cadillac came to making a sports car—was delivered to Mr. Kinney the next day.

Elvis's magnanimity was as big as his purchasing power, which was as big as his appetite. They all go together: his ability to eat, buy, give. His was a life that was truly King size.

The Cadillac Elvis gave his mother. It was the one car he kept
throughout his life. Even after Gladys died, when Gilded Elvis
favored Mercedes limousines and Ferraris, the pink sedan
remained at Graceland, like an eternal flame with tail fins.

Normal standards of measurement go out the window whenever anyone attempts to describe the actual dimensions of Elvis the man, or the real achievements of Elvis the artist.

Many descriptions of him late in his career, when he was at his peak weight, imply that a fork lift was needed to hoist him onstage. In the last few years of his life, he inflated from a trim 185 pounds to 230, 240, maybe even 250—too big to look good, far from the lean sex symbol he had been from 1956 to the early seventies.

But think about it: two and a half C's is hardly freak-show material. Even at his fattest, Elvis bore the physique of a fairly ordinary middle-aged man with a paunch. He could have been any trucker you see hefting his bulk off a stool at the counter in a roadside café —big gut, little butt. (He even adopted the archetypal gear-jammer gesture—hoisting up his slipping pants by their big buckle.)

Nobody ever reveled in the thickening of other male sex symbols—Brando, John Wayne, Frank Sinatra —the way they did in the girth of Elvis. When Elvis turned forty in 1975, tabloids trumpeted the news that he had ballooned to the size of a float in the Macy's Thanksgiving Day parade.

What makes the size of Elvis so abnormally fascinating is the poetic truth of his bloat. As he swelled, so did his music. When, finally, his shows had become as grandiloquent as grand opera and his voice as mighty as a *primo tenore*'s, he truly looked the part, as formidable as Pavarotti or Caruso. The lure of exaggeration is irresistible when dealing with a man whose life was bigger than normal in every other way.

Consider the bare facts: one billion records sold, more than anybody else. Lifetime gross of $4.3 billion. Consider the fact that his television special "Aloha from Hawaii" was watched by half the population of the earth.

Now listen to people trying to measure his talent with words. Rock and roll's premier record producer, Phil Spector, said, "Gosh, he's so great. You have no idea how great, really you don't. You have no comprehension . . . it's absolutely impossible. I can't tell you why he's so great, but he is. He's sensational."

The Smithsonian Institution called him "the single greatest event in the two-hundred-year history of American music."

Hollywood columnist May Mann, in her shocking memoir called *Elvis, Why Won't They Leave You Alone?*, quotes an unidentified starlet as confiding to her that "nature had not only endowed Elvis with talent and a beautiful body, but with a tremendous physical sex organ—that throbbed with heat and energy, as I believe no woman has ever experienced."

Even the meanest detractors never try to make him seem small. They make him *hugely* awful. His temper was Mephistophelean, his gluttony was of Brobdingnagian proportions. His drug use, gloats biographer Albert Goldman, was "enough to stun an elephant."

In the trophy room of Graceland, where many of Elvis's jumpsuits are displayed, the question most commonly asked of guides is: "Have the clothes been taken in?" They have not; but no one can imagine that Elvis Presley fit into garments that look so normal sized.

Elvis's Pantry

Elvis's shopping list was formidable. It was fixed, absolute, unchangeable. In the 1960s, Marty Lacker, foreman of the Memphis Mafia, wrote out an exact inventory of what Elvis required in every circumstance. At the Elvis Hall of Fame in Gatlinburg, Tennessee, Marty's hand-written lists, complete with doodles and charts detailing each man's precise responsibilities, have been mimeographed and are on sale at the souvenir shop. The following things were "to be kept in kitchen and house for Elvis—AT ALL TIMES—EVERY DAY."

1. fresh, lean, unfrozen ground round meat
2. one case regular Pepsi
3. one case orange drinks
4. rolls (hot rolls—Brown 'n' Serve)
5. cans of biscuits (at least six)
6. hamburger buns
7. pickles
8. potatoes and onions
9. assorted fresh fruits
10. cans of sauerkraut
11. wieners
12. at least three bottles of milk and 1/2 & 1/2 cream
13. thin, lean bacon
14. mustard
15. peanut butter
16. fresh, hand-squeezed cold orange juice
17. banana pudding (to be made each night)
18. ingredients for meat loaf and sauce
19. brownies (to be made each night)
20. ice cream—vanilla and chocolate
21. shredded coconut
22. fudge cookies
23. gum (Spearmint, Doublemint, Juicy Fruit—3 each)
24. cigars (El Producto Diamond Tips & El Producto Altas)
25. cigarettes
26. Dristan
27. Super Anahist
28. Contac
29. Sucrets (antibiotic red box)
30. Feenamint gum
31. matches (four to five books)

Wherever Elvis was—in his den, in his car, in a movie theater—he was always accompanied by one member of the Memphis Mafia carrying a cigar box filled with the following:

1. wood-tipped cigars
2. plain cigars
3. tube of Blistex
4. Tareyton cigarettes (two packs)
5. small bottle of Dristan
6. small bottle of Super Anahist
7. one card package of Contac
8. one tin of antibiotic Sucrets
9. two small bottles of eyedrops
10. two emery boards and fingernail file
11. matches
12. one jar of Occuline eye pads (in Los Angeles only)
13. gum
14. sour balls
15. gloves and sunglasses

Bathroom Scales
This set of gold bathroom scales was used by Elvis in his bathroom at Graceland. During the last few years of Elvis' life, he developed a serious weight problem, and therefore became very conscious of his appearance, especially his weight. Elvis used these scales almost every day of the week to monitor those pounds gained or lost.

Graceland

Other than the White House, Graceland is the most recognizable private home in America. And it didn't take two hundred years of history to make it so. Elvis did it all himself.

No song he recorded, no movie he made, nothing Elvis ever did so thoroughly expresses his artistic sensibilities as does this mansion on a hill in Memphis, Tennessee.

Forget tourist attractions like Twitty City and Dollywood and Loretta Lynn Land: they're cookie-cutter celebrity shrines, about as true to the spirit of their namesake's art as each McDonald's is to the personality of its franchisee.

And let's face it: most deceased celebrities' homes are boring. Here's the parlor, there's the study, that's the desk where Famous Person worked. Ho hum. You have to work hard to imagine anybody really living there.

Not at Graceland. Elvis oozes from this place. Every inch of it, every smell, every muffled sound is *his*. No matter that it's been tidied up a bit since his demise, and velvet ropes keep visitors from pawing at the furniture: Elvis is *here*. We know. When we were in the trophy room after hours one night in 1986, we heard his maid, Nancy Rooks (still on the payroll), chatting with "Mr. P" as she strolled among the displays with her dust rag and can of Pledge. She appeared to be all alone, but she told us that Mr. P had assured her he'd come back. So she chats with him as she works.

We're not going to tell you any ghost stories, and we won't go into how the lights inexplicably flickered or

how his guitar strings plunked themselves when we were there alone late that night. But we will tell you this: no home we have ever visited, private or public, asserts the personality of its owner more aggressively than Graceland.

Elvis bought it in March 1957, when he outgrew the ranch house on Audubon Drive (and after neighbors—driven crazy by round-the-clock fans—pleaded for him to go). Inspired by the homestead on which his fictional family lived in his first movie, *Love Me Tender*, he suggested to his mother, Gladys, that they find a farm. She loved the idea: a place where she could have chickens and hogs, and with lawn enough for all the Cadillacs that were crowding the driveway. Graceland was not exactly a working farm, but after they moved in, Elvis drove into the country and came back with his Cadillac limo full of flapping hens, geese, ducks, and peacocks for the backyard.

"When I get it like I want it," twenty-two-year-old Elvis proclaimed when he purchased the hewn fieldstone-fronted mansion, "this is going to be a lot nicer than Red Skelton's house." (Red's hilltop manse in Hollywood had an eleven-car garage and a mile-and-a-half-long driveway.) What an audacious showplace Graceland would be—designed by the same A-bomb sensibility that had just detonated American music.

Built in 1939 and named for Grace Toof, the former owner's great-aunt, Graceland had eighteen rooms, a four-car garage, and a yard full of mature trees and plantings. The land had originally been a Hereford cat-

Graceland's music gates were built for Elvis in 1957 by John Dillars, Sr., of Memphis's Doors, Inc. Right: The living room during its first red period in the 1960s.

tle farm; when the Presleys moved in, Whitehaven (not yet incorporated into Memphis) was still rolling country. The house ("one of Shelby County's most impressive," according to a *Press-Scimitar* story in 1957) had been on the market quite some time. It was used as an annex by a local church and had been offered to the Memphis YMCA in early 1957 for $40,000. For Elvis Presley the price—for the home and fourteen acres of surrounding land—was a cool $100,000.

He planned a bedroom suite all in black, with white leather trim and a white shag rug; twinkle lights and clouds would hover on the ceiling in the central hallway; the living room would be swathed in gold-trimmed purple wallpaper and white corduroy drapes. Batteries of blue and gold spotlights were mounted outside to make the house look as if it glowed in the dark. Within six months, he spent five hundred thousand dollars remodeling.

Like an artist who devotes a lifetime to a magnum opus, Elvis never stopped redecorating Graceland. For twenty years he built new rooms, bulldozed outbuildings, transformed, gutted, and renovated. The result is an environment that could have been put together only by the man whose singing career encompassed "Money Honey," "Rock-a-Hula Baby," and "My Way."

One thing that always stayed the same was the iron gates he installed in 1957 (despite their having to be repaired many times as a result of Elvis's crashing through impatiently). The insignia on the gates—music notes and mirror-image silhouettes of a rockin' guitar man—was Elvis's first coat of arms, a straightforward announcement of who lived here, before the more cryptic heraldry of TCB.

Once the gates are open, the view up the curving driveway is of an antebellum façade, its focal point a massive portico supported by four white Corinthian columns. It is a handsome tribute to Dixie—gracious and old-fashioned, of relatively modest proportions. In fact, by size alone—about ten thousand square feet in the original, unamended structure—Graceland scarcely earns the title "mansion."

But no other term is appropriate. "Mansion" derives from "manor," meaning the residence plus the domain over which the lord rules. Like Hugh Hefner, the other conspicuous mansion-dweller of the modern era, Elvis made his home into a world apart, with its own style and code of behavior and a flip-flop inversion of night and day. Furthermore, the modern connotation of "mansion"—let's be frank—is more of cash than of cul-

A rare white Christmas, 1957. Elvis liked all his cars lined up in the driveway, keys in the ignition, ready to roll.

ture. Old money lives in castles and palaces, or if you want to be understated about it, in homes and cottages. Self-made people, when they get rich, move into mansions. Mansions are where new money lives.

In Elvis's case, he was proud of how new his money was. Graceland's decor is an ode to purchasing power. Every stick of furniture and objet d'art, every car out back, each precious bibelot on display was bought brand-new, in many cases made exclusively for Elvis. He hated antiques. They reminded him of being poor.

The first thing that hits you inside Graceland is the smell. It is a familiar aroma, like a freshly scrubbed

hotel room. It is the cool, syrup-sweet scent of the southern housekeeper's favorite cleanser, Pine Sol, accented with a soupçon of Pledge (regular, not lemon scent). It is a dizzying perfume, an olfactory manifesto that this world wants nothing to do with the natural one outside.

Sequestration is reinforced by stunning quiet, save the whoosh of air conditioners. Windows do not open; some are permanently boarded up. No sound and little light are allowed in.

You could say it is merely an extremist's variation of the need in this climate to create a shelter from the sun and humid air. On the other hand, look around. The mise-en-scène of Graceland conforms to no logic of climate or custom. It is a fantastic vision of wealth, rendered in the insolent style that was Elvis's alone.

The measure of his success is just how viscerally affecting Graceland is. No sentient human can walk through and be unmoved. Understatement, subtlety, clarity, harmony, integrity of materials, comfort: forget those decorating clichés! With a thoroughness never achieved in his nastiest rock-and-roll songs or in his loudest Las Vegas costumes, Elvis has here designed the ultimate challenge to convention, uncensored by any designer's notion of what is appropriate.

"Good taste," "bad taste," "kitsch": such small terms do not do justice to Graceland. This house is too far out to be circumscribed. It is a black hole in the aesthetic universe, where ordinary standards vanish.

The living and dining rooms are vaguely familiar: mottled mirrors, chandeliers, stained-glass peacocks, heavy blue drapes trimmed with gold, white rug and white upholstered furniture. You have seen this place before, but not in the real world. You have seen it in the movies. Only movie sets have such frank semiosis. It says "rich person's home." Remember *Imitation of Life?* Lana Turner could have lived here, in Technicolor.

The view from Elvis's chair at the mirrored dining table, through the living room, toward the gold piano in the music room.

Actually, the formal rooms are subdued compared to the way Elvis had it when he died. The blue-and-gold scheme is pre-1974, reinstated as an *hommage* to the 1960s and 1970s when Elvis and Priscilla were still together, when blue was his favorite color.

At the end of his life, Graceland was red. After Priscilla left, Elvis and his girlfriend Linda Thompson did the front formal rooms in red: red rugs, red satin drapes, and distressed French provincial furniture with blood-red upholstery. "Elvis and Linda were very free-spirited people," interior designer Bill Eubanks told us, "like two children running in and out of stores buying what they liked. Elvis would call me and say, 'Bill, I can't wait for you to see what we did.' I would see it, and swallow hard. There was really no way I could say, 'Oh, Elvis, you have made an abortion!' Graceland is definitely Elvis's house, not my house. Nobody could ever make Elvis's taste anything but what it was."

Bill does take credit for the TV room in the basement, although it was Elvis's idea to brand the supergraphic TCB lightning bolt on the wall. Elvis also insisted that the room be designed around his LBJ-inspired wall unit, with its bank of three televisions. The room has a gas-burning fireplace, plaster animal-horn trophies, and a bar stocked with spring water, Pepsi, and Gatorade (the latter a special favorite because it quenches thirst *fast*—TCB!). Before Elvis added the trophy room, this was where he kept his gold records. The TV room epitomizes a groovy moment in time: early-seventies mod op art, mirrored ceiling, super-stuffed furniture, and a color scheme of navy blue and happy-face yellow.

The pool room also shows Bill Eubanks's hand, although it was Elvis who chose the fin-de-siècle pleated cotton fabric (all 350 yards) that drapes the walls and ceiling. The mood is nostalgic, although everything is new, rather like a ritzy version of the beer sign replicas that people like to put in their rec rooms.

Both of the basement rooms used to have windows, but they were covered up in order to seal everything else out. Each is a separate environment with its own style. One is reminded of how facile Elvis was as a singer, able to slide from low-down blues to ballads or to sing sacred music with unholy ardor. Likewise, he was too restless to have Graceland conform to a single motif. How drab that would have been! How much more fun to have every kind of way-out room you could think of, all in one big house.

The pièce de résistance at Graceland is known as

Although he was known as the rock and roller with a guitar, it was at the piano Elvis sang his favorite religious songs. Those who overheard him singing gospel in moments when he thought he was alone said it was the most beautiful music he ever made. Here he relaxes in the music room, which Graceland's original owners, Dr. and Mrs. Moore, built for their daughter, a harpist with the Memphis Symphony Orchestra.

the jungle room, or as Elvis referred to it, "the den area." Here is Elvis being Elvis to the max, having fun, flaunting his extremism, doing things few of us timid middle-class souls would ever dare . . . or ever even want to dare.

The jungle room was a moment's whim, meaning it was Elvis at his best. (Elvis art is quick art. All of his great songs were chosen based on a fast first impression of a demo.) Legend says he saw an ad on television for a furniture store in Memphis called Donald's. He was amused. He went to Donald's and in thirty minutes picked out the whole room. It was delivered that day: hand-carved pine island-god thrones seven feet tall, distressed and varnished wiggle-edge cypress tables, fake fur lampshades atop wooden lamps carved to resemble angry Tiki gods, couches with gargoyles for arms, rabbit-fur pillows, a mirror framed in pheasant-breast feathers. (The green shag rugs on the ceiling and the illuminated waterfall were already in place.)

A whole room, in one swallow. It was like winning the big curtain on "Let's Make a Deal." No labored planning, no consulting with designers, no swatches of fabric to study. No indecision, no restraint.

This is not to say the jungle room was without precedent in Elvis's oeuvre. Consider his movies *Blue Hawaii* and *Paradise, Hawaiian Style*, and the "Aloha from Hawaii" television concert. Elvis had a special relationship with Hawaii and with the tropical style of the Island State. In fact, along with Trader Vic, he was one of America's great champions of the much-maligned ersatz aesthetic known as Polynesian. (Don't be concerned that Hawaii and Polynesia are different places. We aren't talking geography here; it is a matter of style.)

Hawaii is just about the only place in the U.S.A. that has a tradition of royalty and ceremony to which gilded Elvis could relate. Realities of island life aside, mythological Hawaii (as seen in his movies) was an Elvis ideal: exotic but American, primitive but ornate, and always playful. Unlike his native South, where the rituals of kingship are bound up with social status and stifling traditions, Hawaii glows with the eternal promise of the West, of America at its best: it is wide open; anything goes.

Graceland is the work of a person who believed in such myths and who was uninhibited enough—and rich enough—to fashion his world out of them.

When life became painful for Elvis, it was to this self-created world that he retreated. Gradually, in the

In 1974, Elvis and girlfriend Linda Thompson (Miss Tennessee) decorated the formal rooms Valentine's Day red and turned the pool room into an art nouveau tent. Above: Frolicking on the flotaki with Linda is Git-Lo, Elvis's pet chow. From his first visit to Hawaii in 1957 (right), he relished island life, except for one thing—the heat. Three window air conditioners were installed in the Jungle Room to assist Graceland's central air in lowering the temperature to near-hibernation level. Far right: Polynesia, Presley style, as seen in the Jungle Room, created by Elvis on a thirty-minute shopping spree.

If you want to pronounce "Graceland" correctly—the way Elvis did—stress the first syllable, swallow the second α, and drop the d.

final years, it became his whole world—the only place, other than onstage in concert, where he felt secure. It was in the jungle room that Elvis—unwilling to venture out to an RCA studio—recorded his last two albums.

It was at Graceland that he died on August 16, 1977. And it is here that he is buried—in the meditation garden beyond the swimming pool. When people come to Graceland, they aren't just visiting Elvis Presley's former home; they are with him at his final resting place.

"This is where Elvis is!" one fan disbelievingly exclaimed as we stood over the tablet that clearly marks his grave. Stating the obvious—that Elvis is buried in Elvis's tomb—was no mere recitation of a historical fact. Because Elvis was so unapproachable in life, it is a staggering reality to be so close to him in death. "All that he was," the emotion-racked pilgrim continued, "it is all right here. Elvis is here."

Q & A

These are some of the questions most frequently asked by visitors to Graceland, followed by the answers tour guides give.

WHO OWNS GRACELAND?
It is held in trust for Lisa Marie Presley, who will inherit it when she turns twenty-five [1993].

WILL LISA MARIE CLOSE GRACELAND?
We don't know.

DOES ANYBODY LIVE HERE?
Yes: Elvis's aunt, Delta Mae Biggs.

WHERE DID ELVIS DIE? HOW?
In the master suite of Graceland, on the morning of August 16, 1977, Elvis died of cardiac arrhythmia. He did have a problem with prescription drugs, but the medical examiner concluded that his was not a "drug" death, as insinuated by the press. The amount of drugs (all prescribed), according to the medical examiner, was within prescribed levels; they could not have, individually or in combination, brought on his sudden death. Elvis Presley did not die of a drug overdose.

IS HE REALLY BURIED HERE?
Yes. [There is confusion because Elvis was originally interred alongside his mother at the Forest Hill Ceme-tery. Shortly afterwards (October 2, 1977), Vernon had both their bodies moved to the meditation garden at Graceland.]

WHERE ARE HIS CADILLACS?
He drove a Stutz and a Ferrari. He gave away Cadillacs.

WHY DID HE LIVE IN A BUSINESS AREA?
When he moved here, it was open land.

HOW MUCH LAND IS THERE?
The mansion sits on 13.8 acres. Elvis later bought 11 acres across the street, where the *Lisa Marie* jet plane now stands. He talked of building a movie theater there.

WHY IS THE HOUSE SO SMALL?
In 1957, to a boy from Tupelo and North Memphis, it was a palace. Graceland was "home" and "family" to Elvis. Its size reflects that.

HOW MUCH IS GRACELAND WORTH?
It is priceless . . . just like him.

Looking at Elvis— A Portrait Portfolio

I f all the photographs made of Elvis on stage were gathered together with those in which he posed with fans or celebrities," writes Patsy Hammontree in her scholarly *Elvis Presley, A Bio-Bibliography*, "they could fill a dozen boxcars from floor to ceiling."

Patsy's proposition is an understatement. The world's supply of Elvis pictures couldn't likely be contained in a dozen boxcars, or a hundred. And if you ever did find a freight train long enough to hold all of them, they still couldn't be contained, because fans hungry to look at his face would tear the train apart.

Cameras were fascinated by Elvis. They did not invariably love him, but there was always something thrilling to see.

Can there be any doubt that he was the most photographed man in history? Every time he walked onstage, cameras clicked like a sudden infestation of crickets. Flashguns ignited and didn't stop until he was led offstage—blinded by the light—at the end of the show. Perhaps close to a million separate pictures were taken at every concert; there were a thousand concerts in the last seven years. That's a billion shots right there—many of them duped a hundred times over and disseminated among the faithful.

He never passed through the gates of Graceland without lenses poking at him. When he rode his horse, drove his car, or went to the dentist, he was stalked by fans with Instamatics and by self-appointed "photographers to the King" armed with 500mm mirrored tele-

photos and ultrafast emulsions. When he died, the *National Enquirer* paid five thousand dollars for a sneaked snap of him in his coffin.

But here is a paradox: Elvis was one of the most underphotographed celebrities of modern times. There is no end to the blurry candid shots, taken from the fiftieth row of the concert hall or from the foot of his driveway by shutterbugs on an Elvis safari; but where are the important portraits, the landmark photo sessions with Richard Avedon or Annie Leibovitz? They never happened. Once he became famous, Elvis never had a formal sitting with a great photographer.

RCA, his own record company, was so cavalier about maintaining a picture file that they had to scrounge a photo from collector Jimmy Velvet to have something fresh to use on a recent issue of "Hound Dog" and "Let's Play House." As he toured in the 1970s, there were no photographers among the royal retinue; virtually the only pictures that exist of the last seven years of Elvis's life were snapped by fans and paparazzi. If the Colonel's men spotted someone at a Las Vegas table with professional equipment, his film was confiscated.

Cameras were snuck into concerts inside purses with cutouts for lenses, under giant hats, behind wide ties. The trophies—new pictures of Elvis—fetched enough to support several photographers who spent their lives doing nothing but dogging him, driving all night between concert cities or sneaking onto airport runways to photograph his plane taking off.

The boy from Tupelo (above) lived five years at Memphis's Lauderdale Courts Housing Projects (right) until at age nineteen (below) he sat for his first publicity photo, complete with sneer and sideburns. At far right, "The boy's hair looked as if it had been cut with a lawn mower," said

Memphis *Press-Scimitar* columnist Edwin Howard, when he interviewed Elvis on July 27, 1954. "That's All Right (Mama)," Elvis's first record, had just been released; and in this—his first press photo—he looks more like the truck driver he was than the rock idol he was about to become.

Among the snatched images, there is a hierarchy of worth. Ass shots—Elvis bending over, or walking away from the camera—are the most coveted. Pictures of him licking his lips, sweating, or pointing at the camera are especially valuable. One shutterbug managed to snap a shot of Elvis from the waist down, showing the clear outline of an erection in his pants. The picture was labeled and sold as "IT." Sean Shaver, unofficial court photographer and author of *Elvis—Photographing the King*, fumes that one publisher wanted to know "if I had any photos of Elvis going to the bathroom, or even better, nude."

While most connoisseurs of the Elvis image prefer to see him in a more spiritual light, virtually any never-before-seen picture is prized by fans and collectors, even if it is only a minor variation of an already published one.

Access to Elvis's image can sometimes be daunting. Alfred Wertheimer, a New York photographer who took thirty-eight hundred pictures of Elvis in 1956, charges two thousand dollars *to look at* his proof sheets; if you want to buy a shot, the minimum purchase price is five thousand dollars. The Memphis *Commercial Appeal*, which recorded Elvis's career from the very beginning, has had its entire Elvis archive stolen over the years, piece by piece. At the Memphis Public Library, in order to look at the 1953 Humes High School

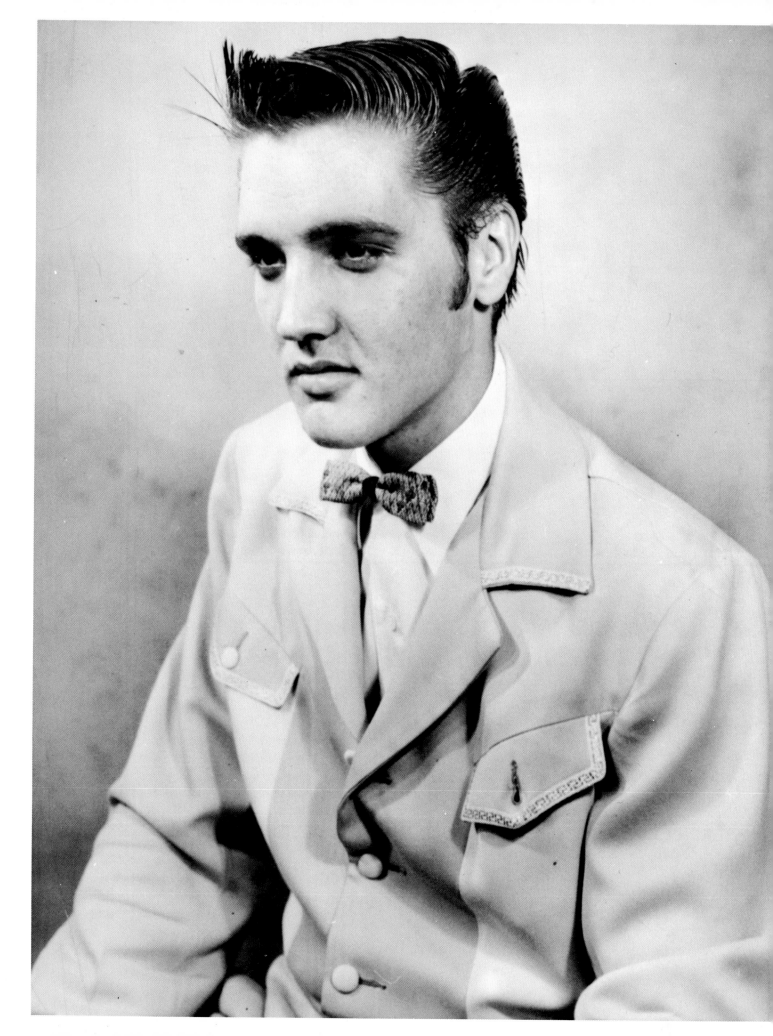

Herald, the yearbook with Elvis Presley's graduation picture, you must supply the librarian with your driver's license or ID "of equal value" before she will fetch it from its locked cage.

Pictures of young Elvis convey a woozy imbalance. He is too intense, or sometimes he is elusive, smirking about something he knows but the camera does not. It is never anything shocking, but some element always seems to be off-kilter. One sock is higher than the other, or his head is tilted funny. His collar is up, his spitcurl is drooping, his lips are slightly apart as if he were whispering endearments to the lens.

Look at the Mississippi boy in his suit jacket at age thirteen, his collar splayed open, hair slicked back short and neat (page 130). The pose is plain, but what about those eyes! They are as focused as a surgeon's who is sewing a vein. Imagine the Tupelo photographer under the black skirt of his studio camera when this kid appeared before him. He must have broken out in a sweat from the force of that stare.

Most early pictures show him alone. Even when he is with others, it isn't difficult to see loneliness in those black-socketed eyes gazing into some private space. Elvis was an only child who would be torn throughout his life between a need for privacy and a craving to be surrounded by friends and admirers.

He stood for the camera the way all children do: the little soldier in his ROTC uniform, the cowboy with pistol and earmuffs. But unlike most goofy kids, he isn't smiling much. He looks purposeful. He is busy sketching, trying poses for some yet-unknown role he is going to play.

That is what is most interesting about the evolution of Elvis portraits: watching him create himself.

He was a teenage dandy who favored pegged pants and two-tone shirts and low-crown hats with a flaring brim. He created his hairstyle based on Tony Curtis's matinee-idol forelock and truck driver's sideburns. He perfected insolence, in the form of his lopsided sneer; he practiced posing with his arms crossed and head tilted back like some arrogant conqueror.

Elvis reached for the dark hair dye, knowing that as a natural blond, he looked washed out. After being intensely photographed for two years in '55 and '56, his

The Lost Photo Session of 1956

Except for an early radio jingle on behalf of Southern Maid Doughnuts, Elvis never endorsed a product. But in 1956, the Hungerford Company, makers of walnut and mahogany furniture, asked him to pose with their latest cabinetry. Bill Carrier, Jr., and Bill Kingdon of API Photographers in Memphis shot these pictures for a proposed advertising campaign. However, when Hungerford's sales managers saw the rock provocateur squatting in front of their product and a paint-by-numbers oil, they nixed the idea. Teenage girls, they figured, were interested in saving their pennies more for Love Me Tender lipstick than for mahogany bureaus; nor would parents be eager to purchase a bedroom suite recommended by a swivel-hipped sex symbol.

The ads never ran, and the pictures were stashed in Graceland's basement and the API archives until 1986.

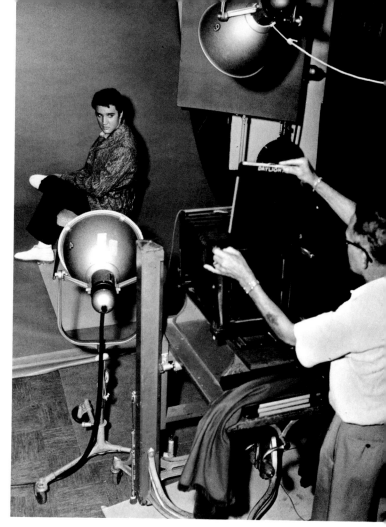

hair was dyed dark, darker, darkest—finally arriving at blue-black, cartoon black, as inky as Superman's or Captain Marvel's locks, all the better to accent the intensity of his blue eyes.

He was never fully satisfied with the results; there was always something about his looks that bothered him. He didn't like his legs, hated them exposed in movie beach scenes. He tolerated no implication he had "love handles," so each movie shirt was cut in such a way that it appeared to hug an all-muscle torso. When he went swimming—in the ocean or a pool—he liked to wear a shirt to cover up. He deemed his neck too long and skinny, and so favored the camouflage of high collars. Getting fat pained him so much that late in life he refused to be measured by his tailors. They had to guess when they made an outfit, and keep guessing until they got it right.

Elvis told Arlene Cogan, author of *Elvis, This One's for You*, that he got the idea of covering Graceland's walls with mirrors when he saw the inside of a ballet studio. It was perfect for self-monitoring every move. Patsy Lacker, co-author of *Elvis: Portrait of a Friend*, recalls Elvis standing up in mid-conversation, walking to a mirror, and saying—apropos of nothing—"I'm pretty, look at that profile." Another time, in the midst of a temper tantrum, as he stormed through the house knocking over lamps and kicking tables, he caught a glimpse of himself in a mirror, stopped still, and exclaimed to his reflection: "You handsome thing, you!" . . . then continued with his fit of rage. Even Elvis was not immune to his own charisma.

Just as he was torn between self-adoration and self-doubt, so he was both exhibitionist and recluse. He complained that he felt like an animal in a zoo, yet he couldn't stand not being noticed. His bodyguards recall the time Elvis sought to disguise himself to accompany Memphis cops on a drug bust. He wore a jumpsuit under a ski suit, his face covered by a ski mask and sunglasses, with a large cigar sticking out the mouth hole. Nobody but Elvis could have devised such attention-grabbing camouflage.

Lew Eliot, of Memphis's Supercycle, where Elvis bought his customized Harley-Davidson trikes, told us that one day when Elvis was sitting around the shop shooting the breeze, his face masked by large sunglasses, a girl walked in and timidly asked, "Are you *him*?" Elvis shook his head no. She left, but he couldn't sit still. As soon as she hit the sidewalk, he jumped up, ran out, and reassured her: "Yeah, honey, I'm Elvis."

Elvis's face, like Garbo's or Marilyn Monroe's, was made for the camera—a great enigma that draws you in but leaves you wanting more. Fill in the blank: it is a face to be feared or mothered; the face of a slick stud or a kid brother, a spacey bopper or a gospel man. He is always Elvis, no doubt about that, but each portrait seems to suggest that Elvis is something different.

If there is any doubt that he was serious about creating his image, look at his first studio portrait out of high school. It was taken in 1954, before he cut a record or sang anywhere for pay. Nonetheless, he figured it was time to get a publicity picture. So he went to Blue Light Studio on Beale Street. Blue Light was (still is) a walk-in, all-purpose storefront shop specializing in brides, grooms, and silver anniversary couples.

The Blue Light picture (page 130) is far from a photographic masterwork, but all the basics of the Elvis look are fully realized: the curled lip, the waterfall of hair, the sideburns, the weird clothes. There is a no-nonsense clarity about the set of his features. In fact, the raw "passport picture while you wait" aesthetic of Blue Light was perfect for showcasing the visual force of early Elvis—exactly as the crude Sun Studio recordings captured the youthful thrill of his voice. (Ten years later, in 1963, Blue Light would be where Priscilla reached her teen peak in the monumental beehive hairdo photos.)

By the middle of 1955, Elvis's musical career was zooming. But if he was ever going to realize his dream of becoming a movie star, he needed a portfolio more substantial than the Blue Light picture. Bob Neal, his manager then, brought him to the studio of William Speer to get glossies that could be sent out to Hollywood.

Speer was a glamour photographer, originally from Fort Worth, who had come to Memphis from Hollywood in the late 1940s. His session with Elvis in June 1955 was the first—and arguably the *only*—serious photographic sitting Elvis ever had.

When Elvis arrived at the studio, Speer was in the darkroom. His wife, Vacil, a sexy Mediterranean brunette, met the twenty-year-old boy at the door. "I looked him over head to toe," she recalls. "And he did the same to me. There was strong electricity in Elvis. Magnetism."

One can only guess what young Elvis Presley must have thought of the Speers. He knew little about life outside of the familiar South; they, on the other hand, were bohemians, stylish artistes for whom photography was a means of exoticizing the world. William Speer favored berets and wore a goatee. Vacil—who according to her husband is the reincarnation of Cleopatra—had jet-black, waist-length hair, slave bracelets on her upper arms, and a traffic-stopping cleavage.

"What impressed me," Speer said about the rockabilly singer he photographed that summer, "was the fact that he looked like a young Burt Lancaster." (In fact, Elvis's screen test, a year later, was for a role in *The Rainmaker* alongside Lancaster.) "The other thing I recall about that day was that he couldn't sit still. He was strumming and fidgeting and moving about so much I hardly had time to change apertures."

It was Vacil who suggested Elvis take his shirt off for some of the pictures. The Speers were accustomed to

In 1955, at age twenty, Elvis had Memphis photographer William Speer shoot the following pictures in hopes of seducing Hollywood and becoming a movie star.

Now supported by their successful son, Elvis's happy parents followed him into Speer's studio.

shooting female nudes, and there was something about Elvis, they recall, that inspired the same sexy approach. Elvis said he was embarrassed, but went along. The next day, he sent his parents to the Speer studio to have their picture taken, too. "Vernon was shocked when I told him it would cost a hundred and fifty dollars for the photograph," Speer says. "He thought I was overcharging them just because of who their son was."

A few days after the sitting, at the Loew's Theater in Memphis, Elvis ran into the Speers in the lobby and wanted to know how the pictures had turned out. But he was shy talking to Mr. Speer. "You don't like me," he said nervously, "so I guess I better talk to your wife." When he looked at the proofs, he wrote a note on the back of each of the bare-chested ones, saying, "I don't want this one!"

"I never photographed him again," Speer told us.

"But I used to see him later on, driving around Memphis on his motorcycle. You know, when he got old and let his hair grow long, he looked just like his mother."

The picture that was selected as the official publicity shot for the first few years of Elvis's career is one of the strangest pictures ever taken of him—strange because, for once in his life before the lens, he almost doesn't look like Elvis.

He is instead a swarthy, Latinate lover boy. (In fact, several early articles erroneously describe him as part Italian, which was the reigning nationality in the mid-1950s for singers who made girls' hearts flutter.) He is uncharacteristically sincere in this pose, his hands clasped earnestly by the side of his head. His gaudy watch appears—in this sedate context—to be a charm bracelet, perhaps a girlfriend's.

His eyes are dark, far away instead of reckoning

with the camera. His hair is curly, a little mussed but not frighteningly wild, without grease, without a wave on top, the sideburns obscured. His sincerity is reinforced by a firm-set jaw.

The Speers are strange photographs because despite Elvis's nervous agitation in the studio, they still him. They are beautiful studies of a beautiful boy, but something is missing from them that permeates slap-dash portraits of early Elvis. There is no sneer, no curled lip, no irony. Elvis isn't having the fun time he seems to have before the lens in less structured photo situations.

Comparing the head-on Blue Light portrait with the artistic Speers, the inevitable conclusion is that the dearth of "important" studio portraits is no accident. Elvis exuded Elvisness best in the same way he sang best—quickly, off the cuff, without a lot of premeditation.

In the 1950s, when whirlwind success carried him along, all the quickie portraits radiate the pleasure he was having playing at being Elvis. The famous curled lip is definitely a smile, a dash of amusement that underlines the silliness of all this fame and adulation.

Then a strange thing happened in the 1960s. The portraits get very weird. Elvis looks stiff, spiffed up,

trapped by the camera. He is surrealistically perfect, all his famous eccentricities reduced to formulaic elements. His skin has the texture of a nylon stocking; his hair looks like poured tar. The synthetic look is not surprising, since almost all of these pictures were taken as PR for the movies in which he began to feel so awkward.

After 1969, Elvis never again sat for a serious portrait. That year was a turning point in every aspect of his career. He returned to Memphis to record real music again instead of the movie soundtracks that had stifled his voice for a decade. Cameras—movie and still—had become a dead end. Elvis needed to reanimate himself; so he began performing live again for the first time in eight years, trading the sterile Hollywood sound stage for the visceral reaction of an audience.

Most fans will tell you that the magic of Elvis of the 1970s eludes the camera. "You had to be there," they repeat like a litany. And candid concert photos of that era bear them out: it is impossible to sense the enveloping thrill of those performances merely by looking at a single moment captured in a picture. The art of being Elvis had reached a point at which it transcended anything a camera could reveal.

Wonders of Elvis World

The great sights of Elvis World are all in Tupelo and Memphis. His Hollywood and Palm Springs homes, the rental house in Germany, Studio B in Nashville, the Army-days retreat down in Texas that his friend Eddie Fadal has made into a little museum: all were places where Elvis felt away from home, distant satellites to the small part of the earth that he considered his.

First stop on the Elvis trail is in Tupelo, Mississippi: the two-room house on Elvis Presley Drive in Presley Heights. This is where he was born at 4:35 a.m. on January 8, 1935. The street was then called Old Saltillo Road and the Heights were East Tupelo—a separate town on the wrong side of the railroad tracks where poor people lived.

The house was built in 1934 by Elvis's father, Vernon, with help from Elvis's Uncle Vester and grandpa J. D. Presley. Known as a shotgun shack because you could poke a barrel in the front door and the blast would exit clean out the back door, it is a mere 450 square feet, raised up on stone piles to protect it from flooding in the spring. Vernon built a barn and an outhouse; and although East Tupelo was wired for electricity in 1934 (Tupelo was the first town to benefit from the Tennessee Valley Authority rural electrification program), the Presleys lived by oil lamps. In the dirt yard that Gladys swept clean each day, they kept chickens and a cow.

After he became famous, Elvis often returned to his little home. Sarah Parham, librarian at Lawhon School, told us she remembers that in the 1950s "word would get around that Elvis's Lincoln or Cadillac had come to town late at night. He and [girlfriend] Anita Wood went to the house on Old Saltillo Road, they visited his aunt, then walked here to his old school."

Later in his life, the house fell into disrepair, but was saved from ruin by Mrs. Billie Boyd and the East Heights Garden Club. Now it has been thoroughly beautified, its bare boards painted white, walls covered with floral paper, chintz curtains at the windows, and pretty green grass and shrubs all around the outside. There is a souvenir shop in back and a quiet Elvis Presley chapel on a knoll nearby.

For the serious Elvis World pilgrim, Tupelo resonates with meaning, its streets dappled with shadows of Elvis and the Presley family. Here is Lawhon School, where Elvis's classmates called him "Old Super Ears" because he had such sharp hearing he could listen to other people's conversations while keeping up his own separate patter. Lawhon is where Mrs. Grimes coaxed fifth-grade Elvis to get up and sing "Old Shep"—a sad song about a lad who must shoot his dog. Mrs. Grimes thought he sang it so sweetly that she had him perform for the principal, Mr. Cole; and they decided to make Elvis Lawhon's entry in the children's talent contest at the Mississippi–Alabama Fair.

It is a short walk from Lawhon School to the fairgrounds, where a few months after his debut before his classmates, Elvis stood up on a chair and sang "Old Shep" again. Based on grandstand applause, he won second prize, then collected his first earnings as a

In 1935, this shack was new, set on stone piles above mud. Shrubs, walkway, and white paint are recent additions.

singer: five dollars and a free pass to all fair attractions.

On Main Street, you can stop in Long's Dry Cleaners, which now specializes in prewashing jeans to give them a worn look, but still appears exactly as it must have forty years ago, when Vernon and Uncle Vester worked in back, cleaning clothes. Across the street is Leake and Goodlett lumberyard, where Vernon worked for a salary of eighteen dollars a week.

Just up Main Street is the Tupelo Hardware Company. This is where Elvis got his first guitar. Myth says he was given a choice between a bicycle and a guitar for his birthday (either the ninth or tenth), and he chose the latter. That is not the way the late Mr. F. L. Bobo, salesman at Tupelo Hardware in the 1940s, remembered it. Before he died in 1983, Mr. Bobo wrote an affidavit, now framed and posted in the second-floor office of the store, about the First Guitar.

Mr. Bobo's story is that Elvis really wanted a .22 rifle. His mother, Gladys, didn't want him to have the gun. "Elvis cried and cut up, he had a tantrum right here." Gladys and Mr. Bobo tried to calm cranky little Elvis by taking him to the guitar and fiddle section of the store. But Elvis wanted none of it. "If you don't behave," Gladys warned him, grabbing and shaking him by his skinny shoulders, "I'll take you home and give you a spanking instead of a present."

There were three models of guitar: $8.75, $13.75, and $18.75. Elvis got the cheapest. "You take the guitar home and learn something," Mr. Bobo told him. "Someday you may be famous."

How strange it is to stand in this good old southern hardware store and watch busloads of tourists from around the world walk in awestruck. Male fans buy a screwdriver or a roll of duct tape just to have some business here; ladies from Japan dirty their kimonos when they fall to their knees on the very spot of the wood floor where Elvis had the tantrum and first took hold of his guitar.

Out Priceville Road, it is easy to find the cemetery where Elvis's twin brother, Jesse Garon, is buried. There is no marker, because Vernon and Gladys hadn't the money to buy one; but the cemetery holds the graves of many other Tupelo Presleys, and it is said that young Elvis often came here to be close to the stillborn twin with whom he felt a lifelong attachment. It is a lovely place, overgrown with wildflowers in the spring, buzzing with fat bees. And there are many little lamb-shaped tombstones that mark the graves of infants wealthier than Jesse Garon.

Downtown Tupelo has one of the weirdest shrines in Presleydom: a McDonald's franchise stocked with pictures of Elvis from the collection of Presley family friend Janelle McComb and decorated with etched-glass Elvis faces above the condiments. But decoration is where it ends; the restaurant fixtures are standard-issue molded plastic (rather than some uniquely Elvoid theme, such as jungle-room fake fur or rolled and tufted Naugahyde). And the menu is the same as all McDonald's in the land. We got only funny looks from the staff when we asked for our Quarter Pounders extra-extra well done—the way Elvis would have wanted them.

Although it has no specific Elvis sights to see, Route 78 is a hallowed road, because it took the Presleys from Tupelo to Memphis in the autumn of 1948. The move was a fast one; Vernon was in trouble for selling a stolen pig, and he had just been fired as a delivery man. Elvis's classmates at Milam Junior High School requested he perform one last time for them. He sang "Leaf on a Tree," and shortly thereafter, the family piled their possessions into their 1939 Plymouth and headed for the city.

Of the many places the Presleys lived in Memphis, Lauderdale Courts is the important one, because it is where Elvis truly became Elvis. It was a federal housing project built during the Depression and occupied in the late 1940s mostly by single (white) women with families to support. The Presleys, including grandma Minnie Mae, moved to the Courts in 1949 and stayed until they were evicted on January 7, 1953, for having too large an income.

In the Courts Elvis met Bill Black (with whom he would record his first professionally released songs), and the two of them began to jam informally. "The boys who lived in the Courts were jealous of him," recalls Mary Ann, a former neighbor, who was a year older than Elvis and one of his pals. "They called him 'Velvet Lips Presley' and used to chase him. But he was fast. He was the fastest runner I ever saw." She remembers that he never wore jeans, that he liked high-waisted pants "to give himself a shape. He had no legs, a skinny chest, and a big butt." One day he appeared below her window with a permanent wave, wearing his mother's makeup. And she laughs about how often her grandmother shooed him out of their apartment because he hung around all night singing "Lawdy, Miss Clawdy" and banging his guitar.

It is hard to picture young Elvis serenading friends in the Courts as they are today—a frightful slum. The grass yard, once immaculately maintained, is scattered with garbage. The Presleys' two-bedroom apartment faces the concrete roadway of I-40 and houses a family of nine. At night, the walkways among the low-slung brick buildings are ominously quiet.

No one knows for sure how much young Elvis Presley hung around Beale Street, home of the blues and of black nightlife. But it is a certainty his taste in clothing was perfected there. Lansky Brothers is where R&B musicians Rufus Thomas and Little Milton got their sharp threads, and where Elvis learned to love the

combo of pink and black. "He had nothing to wear, he had no clothes at all," says Bernard Lansky in a gravel-rough voice that is equal parts black southern hipster and Jewish shopkeeper. The Lanskys remedied that situation by supplying him with some of the wildest duds ever worn by a white man.

"We knew Elvis from the time he was a forty-two long with a thirty-four-inch waist to forty-six long and forty around the middle," says Willie Clayborne, the six-foot-six black man who is assistant manager of Lanskys. "You could dress that man up like a rag doll and he would still look good; he was that handsome. *Handsome!* He was something to see. He'd come in and I would lay out ten outfits, and he would say 'this' and 'this' and 'this,' and when he couldn't decide, he would take one of everything. He wasn't fussy, but he always asked if he looked good, he always wanted to be told."

Elvis loved shopping at Lansky Brothers, which now specializes in big and tall men's fashions. Branches of Lanskys' are elsewhere, but the Beale Street store is the one that served Elvis, and it has his dressing room and mirror cordoned off like a shrine. In a garage somewhere in Memphis, Bernard Lansky is still storing the three-wheel Messerschmidt car that Elvis exchanged for a shopping spree of indeterminate length.

On the Elvis trail. This 1950s tracker points to what she believes is Elvis's own hand-carved graffiti at Crown Electric Company, where he worked as a teenager.

TUPELO HARDWARE. Owner Billy Booth points to the exact spot where Elvis stood while Gladys bought him the first guitar.

LEAKE AND GOODLETT LUMBER, where Elvis's father worked in 1941 when Elvis was six. It is rumored that Elvis's birthplace was built from wood bought here.

BUSINESS DISTRICT
TUPELO
FIRST T·V·A CITY

LONG'S DRY CLEANERS, where Elvis's father and Uncle Vester worked.

This Tupelo MCDONALD'S is a tribute to Elvis. Hamburgers were always his favorite food.

PRICEVILLE CEMETERY. Here, in an unmarked grave, lies baby Jesse Garon, Elvis's twin brother, who died at birth.

BIRTHPLACE. The Presleys lost the house in 1938, when times got hard.

LAWHON JUNIOR HIGH auditorium, where fifth-grader Elvis sang.

Elvis World Addresses

These are places in Memphis and Mississippi where Elvis lived, shopped, worked, and played. In order to be helpful for self-guided tours of Elvis World, this list is only of shrines still standing.

HOMES

Lauderdale Courts: $35 per month for four rooms and a bath.

1935–37: 306 Elvis Presley Drive (formerly Old Saltillo Road), Tupelo, Mississippi: Elvis's birthplace

1949–53: 185 Winchester Street, Memphis: Lauderdale Courts

1954–55: 2414 Lamar Avenue, Memphis (now a nursery school)

1955–56: 1414 Getwell Road, Memphis

1956–57: 1034 Audubon Drive, Memphis

1957–77: 3764 Elvis Presley Boulevard, Memphis: Graceland

SCHOOLS

Humes High, where Elvis was taunted for his two-tone shirts and flamboyant hair.

Lawhon Junior High, 140 Lake, Tupelo. Formerly East Tupelo Consolidated School, where Elvis sang "Old Shep" to his fifth-grade class.

Milam Junior High, 720 West Jefferson, Tupelo. Elvis attended sixth and seventh grades with his guitar slung over his shoulder.

Humes High School, 659 Manassas, Memphis. "They really liked me," Elvis proclaimed to homeroom teacher Elsie Scrivener after singing in a school talent contest. "They really did like me."

Immaculate Conception Cathedral High School, Central Avenue and Belvedere Boulevard, Memphis. Priscilla went to school here while living at Graceland. She graduated in 1963.

Kang Rhee Institute of Self-Defense, 1911 Poplar Avenue, Memphis. Where Elvis attained his karate black belt.

LIFE AND DEATH

Baptist Memorial Hospital, 1111 Union Avenue, Memphis. Lisa Marie was born here, February 1, 1968. Elvis's body was taken here in an ambulance by the emergency medical team the day he died, August 16, 1977.

Forest Hill Cemetery, 1661 Elvis Presley Boulevard, Memphis. Gladys's burial site in 1958, Elvis's resting place in 1977. Both bodies were moved to the meditation garden at Graceland in October 1977.

Memphis Funeral Home, 1177 Union Avenue, Memphis. Elvis's body was prepared for burial here.

Priceville Cemetery, Priceville Road, outside of Tupelo, Mississippi. The country cemetery where Elvis's still-born twin brother, Jesse Garon, was buried, January 9, 1935. The grave is unmarked.

Elvis used to make late-night visits to the Memphis Funeral Home to ponder the dead.

RELIGION

First Assembly of God Church, 206 Adams Street, Tupelo, Mississippi. The Presley family's first church.

First Assembly of God Church, 255 Highland, Memphis. Elvis's boyhood Sunday school.

The parking lot at 255 Highland, Memphis, a city known as "the buckle on the Bible Belt."

PLAY

Fairgrounds, Tupelo, Mississippi. Where Elvis won second prize in the children's talent contest in 1945 and returned in 1956 for a triumphant homecoming concert.

Libertyland, in the fairgrounds off East Parkway, Memphis. Formerly the Fairgrounds Amusement Park, rented by Elvis at the cost of $14,000 per night.

Memphian Theater, 51 South Cooper, Memphis. Rented out by Elvis for midnight movie parties (now called Playhouse on the Square).

Rainbow Rollerdome, Lamar Avenue and Filmore Avenue, Memphis. Elvis's high-school skating rink. Later he rented it for himself and his friends for all-night sessions of "crack the whip" and "war."

CAR AND MOTORCYCLE DEALERS

Bill Spero,
Madison Cadillac

Fred Woloshyn,
Autorama: "Elvis stood here."

Autorama, 2950 Airways Boulevard, Memphis. Formerly Robertson Motors, where Elvis purchased many Mercedes-Benzes.

Madison Cadillac, 341 Union Avenue, Memphis. "The Cadillac of Cadillac Dealers"; formerly Southern Motors. Elvis's favorite salesman was Howard Massey.

Schilling Lincoln-Mercury, 987 Union Avenue, Memphis. Elvis once bought an entire lotful of Lincolns.

Supercycle, 620 Bellevue Boulevard South, Memphis. Co-owner Lew Eliot chromed and customized many of Elvis's trikes and Harley-Davidsons, also Lisa Marie's golf cart.

FAVORITE PLACES TO SHOP

At the Lansky Brothers store, visitors can look in Elvis's dressing mirror.

Burke's Florist, 1609 Elvis Presley Boulevard, Memphis. Supplied Graceland with floral bouquets.

Goldsmith's Department Store, 123 Mid-America Mall, Memphis. Department store of choice for Christmas shopping sprees; source of mink coats for Gladys, Priscilla, wives of friends, and little Lisa Marie.

Lansky Brothers, 126 Beale Street, Memphis. "Clothier to the King."

Lowell Hays, 4872 Poplar Avenue, Memphis. Favorite diamond dealer, designer-maker of TCB ring, Maltese Cross, much 1970s jewelry.

Poplar Tunes, 308 Poplar Avenue, Memphis. Record store just down the street from Lauderdale Courts, where young Elvis bought his platters.

McCormick-Eubanks Interior Design, Inc., 1793 Union Avenue, Memphis. Bill Eubanks worked with Elvis and Linda Thompson in 1974 redecorating Graceland.

RESTAURANTS

Chenault's, 1402 Elvis Presley Boulevard, Memphis. Elvis and the guys used to hang out in the "Delta Room" in back. Specialty of the house is biscuits and sorghum syrup.

The Gridiron, 4101 Elvis Presley Boulevard, Memphis. Open all night, a favorite source of well-done hamburgers.

Piccadilly Cafeteria, Whitehaven Plaza, Memphis. Where young Priscilla modeled clothes in fashion shows after school.

WORK

Leake and Goodlett, Inc., Lumber, 105 East Main, Tupelo. Vernon worked here as a handyman in 1941.

Long's Dry Cleaners, 130 East Main, Tupelo. Vernon and Uncle Vester cleaned the clothes of fellow Tupelonians in the early 1940s.

Precision Tool, McLemore Avenue and Kansas Street, Memphis. An after-school job for Elvis, until mother Gladys made him quit because he was falling asleep in classes.

United Paint, 404 Mallory Avenue, Memphis. Vernon packed crates: his first job after arriving in Memphis.

American Sound Studios, 827 Thomas, Memphis. Elvis returned to Memphis in 1969 and recorded thirty-five songs here—his best studio work since 1956. Hits from these sessions include "Suspicious Minds," "In the Ghetto," "Don't Cry Daddy," and "Kentucky Rain." (No longer open to the public.)

Sun Records, 706 Union Avenue, Memphis. Elvis's recording career began in this building, at the Memphis Recording Service (a.k.a. Sun Records), in July 1954 (no longer a studio).

OTHER SHRINES

Blue Light Studio, 145 Main Street, Memphis. Elvis's first publicity photo was taken by Blue Light in 1954. In 1964, Priscilla came to Blue Light with her tall bouffant. Owner Lola Blood Caccamisi helped her pose; Margaret Sutton was the photographer. (At the time Blue Light was down the street at Beale and Second.)

Chiska Hotel, Main Street and Linden Avenue, Memphis. Former home of WHBQ, where disc jockey Dewey Phillips first played an Elvis record ("That's All Right") on his "Red Hot and Blue" show, July 7, 1954 (now a church).

Doors, Inc., 911 Rayner, Memphis. The music gates for Graceland were made by Doors, Inc., in 1957.

Ellis Auditorium, Main Street and Exchange, Memphis. Here, Elvis attended all-night gospel sings when he was a boy, and learned to play the piano.

Overton Park Band Shell, Overton Park, Memphis. On July 30, 1954, Elvis first appeared as a featured act, along with Slim Whitman.

Tupelo Hardware, 114 West Main Street, Tupelo. Elvis got his first guitar here, a birthday present from his mother in 1945.

At Lew Eliot's Supercycle, it is easy to imagine what Elvis might have been like had he not become famous. He used to visit Lew's place incognito and relish the luxury of being a plain good ol' boy, drinking Pepsi and palavering about knucklehead Harleys. Lew's roommate's girlfriend styled Priscilla's bouffant in its halcyon days of 1963.

Back in 1956, the Lanskys came to Elvis's defense when the Custom Tailors Guild of America accused him, Marlon Brando, and Ted Williams of being "sloppy celebrities." "He may not be the most conservative dresser in the world," Bernard responded, "but don't let anybody fool you. That kid's a sharp dresser. Some of his outfits are out of this world." He explained, for example, that "every stitch down the sides of Elvis's forty pairs of pegged slacks has to be a contrasting color."

There is no record that Elvis ever set foot inside Broadway Pizza, on Broad Avenue, but it is nonetheless a noted shrine in Elvis World. Here one burps down pepperoni pies surrounded by framed locks of Elvis hair, his karate black belt, and a hundred paintings, drawings, busts, and posters of the King. Dewana Anne Plunk, daughter of proprietor Janet Cox, is a beauty queen and karate star, and her pictures, in ball gowns and black-belt GIs, are featured on the wall along with Elvis's.

Janet Cox is probably a bigger fan than her husband, Doug, but Doug is quick to point out the many similarities between himself and the great man. Doug, like 1977 Elvis, is heavy-set; and although he has a beard and dark eyes and doesn't sing, note the following: "Elvis and I share the same ring size, the same birthday, and we are the same height. And we are both TV fanatics."

In search of Elvis we stopped at Supercycle on Bellevue, the boulevard that leads out to Graceland. Proprietor Lew Eliot, while discussing Elvis's taste in Harley-Davidsons, revealed that he not only outfitted Elvis with motorcycles; he also supplied Elvis and Priscilla with their Black Velvet hair dye. Back in the 1960s, before he started selling cycles, Lew was a Clairol route

man, and his roommate's girlfriend used to style some of those lofty hairdos Priscilla wore.

Elvis liked Lew because he could work magic. Like the December twenty-third when Elvis called to order a chrome-plated golf cart for Lisa Marie. Lew got his chrome platers to work round the clock and delivered the cart in time for Christmas. He remembers another emergency call in the middle of the night: the Lord and Lady of Graceland had run out of hair dye, and they needed him to pack a case and bring it over immediately. He woke his roommate, who got all dressed up to meet Elvis, and the two of them drove out to Graceland. They were met at the back door by Priscilla's mother, who took the Black Velvet and sent them on their way.

It was Lew who suggested that Elvis try riding trikes instead of bikes once he started getting heavy. "Vernon just about died when Elvis pulled up to Graceland in his first trike," Lew laughs. "That one was fitted with a hot VW engine and had a real bad habit of doing wheelies." Lew's voice lowers to reveal a confidence: "Elvis didn't take very good care of his motorcycles. After he died, Graceland called and said his cycles had fallen into disrepair. I told them that was the way they were when he was alive. He treated them like toys."

Elvis liked to hang around Supercycle with his cousins and cronies; and when other customers came in, he would pretend he was the Coca-Cola delivery man, butting into conversations to ask Lew how many cases of pop he wanted. In fact, Supercycle was one of the few public places Elvis could comfortably hang out without getting mobbed. Lew once asked if the constant attention from fans didn't drive him crazy. "No, man," Elvis said, leaning back philosophically in the fringed saddle of one of Lew's Electra-Glides. "That's part of it."

Elvis Hall of Fame

GATLINBURG, TENNESSEE

"See . . . Elvis's Hollywood bedroom.

"See . . . Elvis's first dollar.

"See . . . Items from Elvis's wedding."

See X-rays, checkbook stubs, bathroom scales, a $250,000 diamond TCB ring, a green-enamel ashtray, a toss pillow, Vera bath towels, undershirts, hankies, and many other artifacts from the Life of Elvis, gathered by curator Mike L. Moon.

Souvenirs for sale include photocopies of Elvis's karate school diploma and his weekly shopping list.

Cameras are welcome.

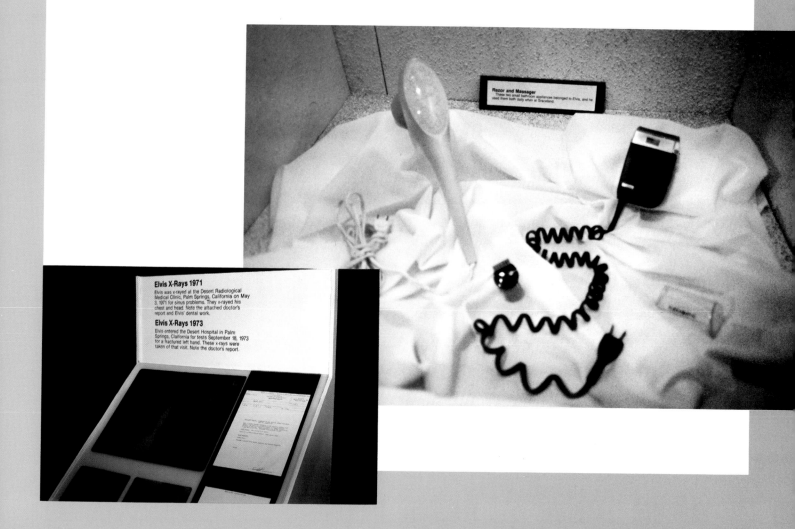

Curator's Choice: Highlights from Jimmy Velvet's Museum

JIMMY VELVET   ELVIS PRESLEY

CARS

1969 MERCEDES-BENZ LIMOUSINE. *Der grosse Pullman*, a six-door Graceland on wheels. Navy blue with blue leather and velvet interior and a solid copper floor. The biggest, fastest, and most expensive limo ever made. Jimmy swears it will go from zero to 150 in under five seconds.

1966 ROLLS-ROYCE SILVER CLOUD III. White with dark blue leather. Bought new by Michael Landon, from whom Elvis purchased it. Subsequently owned by Charlie Rich, then by a couple of doctors in Memphis. Value: $200,000.

1969 MERCEDES-BENZ LIMOUSINE. Silver with black leather interior. Only four doors, smaller than *der grosse Pullman*. Originally owned by David Seville (of Alvin and the Chipmunks). A gift from Elvis to Jimmy Velvet in 1974.

1977 CADILLAC SEVILLE. Maroon with silver leather interior. Elvis's last Cadillac, which Vernon gave to Ginger Alden (Elvis's girlfriend) on August 25, 1977.

JEWELRY

LION CLAW NECKLACE. Fifteen diamonds, two cabochon rubies, and the claw of a black-maned lion (taken by Bill Jeffreys of Beverly Hills). Elvis gave it to Bob Cantwell of the Denver Police Department. Estimated value: $23,000 ("But I wouldn't take $100,000," says Jimmy).

TREE OF LIFE PENDANT. 24-karat gold. A 1964 Christmas gift to Elvis from the guys. All their names are on the branches in English, Hebrew, and Latin; Elvis's is on the trunk. Designed by Marty Lacker and made by Memphis jeweler Harry Levitch.

WEDDING RING. Three rows of diamonds set in platinum. Three days before he died, Elvis was sitting in his bedroom with stepbrother David Stanley and his wife, Angie, who were having marital problems. Elvis gave them his wedding ring in hopes that it would bring them together.

SMILEY FACE RING. Gift from jeweler Harry Levitch to Lisa Marie Presley. Subsequently given by grandmother Minnie Mae Presley to cousin Donna Pritchard.

JAPANESE RING. Diamonds and antique jade. Given to Elvis in 1970 by a Japanese fan club. Then given by Elvis to Captain Kennedy of the Denver Police Department.

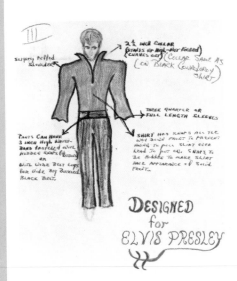

Jimmy bought this sketch for his museum from Marty Lacker.

If you cannot visit the great places in Elvis World, a significant part of Elvis World will come to you, courtesy of Jimmy Velvet. Jimmy is the man behind the Elvis Presley Museum on Tour, a trio of eighteen-wheel semis filled with clothes, cars, jewelry, and personal artifacts—the largest collection of Elvis memorabilia outside of Graceland. Each of the three trucks travels to the malls and shopping centers of America, setting up a display of his things that is attended by as many as a quarter-million people per weekend.

Jimmy Velvet was fourteen when he met Elvis in 1955 in Jacksonville, Florida. Elvis was fourth on a bill featuring Hank Snow, Slim Whitman, and Faron Young. The next year, when the Elvis Presley show came to town and the judge prohibited Elvis from wiggling, Jimmy managed to get backstage. The two became pals, sucking on soft drinks together and talking about things that southern boys talk about. "I think Elvis saw himself in me," Jimmy said. "We were both quiet and polite, we both loved music, we both were not that interested in school."

Because he had his own singing career, Jimmy never became one of the Memphis Mafia, but he occasionally traveled with Elvis, hung around Graceland, and was close enough to be gifted with a car (in this case, a Mercedes limo with a blown engine that cost eight thousand dollars to repair). When Elvis died, Jimmy became incensed that Memphis politicians were quibbling about whether to establish an Elvis Presley Museum, so he did it himself.

It started with twenty-four artifacts in a small Memphis shopping center in 1978. He has since bought and collected a phenomenal amount of Presliana, which he displays in permanent exhibits in Orlando and Honolulu and in the three traveling museums.

When they are not on the road with their museums, Jimmy and his wife, Kathy, live in a ten-thousand-square-foot house in a well-groomed residential area outside of Nashville. Their place is easy to find: it's the one with the semi truck parked in the driveway, along with the Cadillac Seville with a TCB license plate, and Elvis's *Hound Dog* motorboat on a trailer at the iron gates.

Like Elvis, Jimmy and Kathy are not day people, so our visit at the brutal hour of 9:00 a.m. finds them still a bit drowsy in their twin Barcaloungers in the den. We are given similar seats on a couch, which at the touch of

a button reclines and sprouts leg rests. The four of us sit together in perfect postures for dental work, surrounded by Elvis's possessions.

A blue-satin jeweled jumpsuit is draped across a chair. We place our notebook on Elvis's coffee table. His fake fur overcoat is hanging on a banister in the hall. Everywhere one looks, there are Elvis things waiting to be labeled and sent on tour: his pendants, his cufflinks, his report card, his dinner plates, his candlesticks. One must shuffle sideways through the hallway to get past Plexiglas display cases filled with Elvis eyeglasses, his driver's license, and his softball jersey.

The Velvets are generous hosts. While we talk, they bring carrot sticks and pickles to munch, then tuna salad and iced tea, followed by bowls of jade-green pistachio pudding. We eat Elvis-style, in front of a giant-screen television. We drop a glob of tuna only three inches from the blue jumpsuit.

The Velvets' inventory is staggering. They have thirteen cars, 241 pieces of jewelry, Elvis's bed from his Hollywood home, and one of the original pianos from the music room at Graceland. They have cartons full of yet-uncatalogued possessions. There is Elvis's motorcycle out in the back shed; a black opal for which Elvis searched the world; his .357 magnum with fourteen-karat TCB gold grips. It is priceless merchandise, for which Jimmy pays fortunes and which fans across the country are eager to see. Yet its value is oddly artificial. One wonders what price Elvis's toothbrush or tennis shoes would command at a Sotheby's auction.

As we browse through boxes of Presley family Polaroids, report cards, scribblings, and home movies—as cheerfully unkempt as our own unorganized personal files at home—we are struck by just how strange it is that so many of Elvis's personal possessions have wound up here. It is no secret that he loved to give things away, that a favorite ring was favorite only until he was struck by the whim to let someone else enjoy it. But then once Elvis gave them away, his things seem to have made many journeys, sold by those in need, traded and bought by collectors.

"I get ten letters a day from people with something of Elvis's for sale," Jimmy says. Although they have exhibited Elvis's underwear, some relics the Velvets own are not displayed, for the sake of good taste: Elvis's prescriptions, for example. Kathy confides that Jimmy was offered a film of Elvis's autopsy and was tempted to buy it . . . just so he could destroy it. He likes to think of himself as a friend of Elvis first, then as a curator.

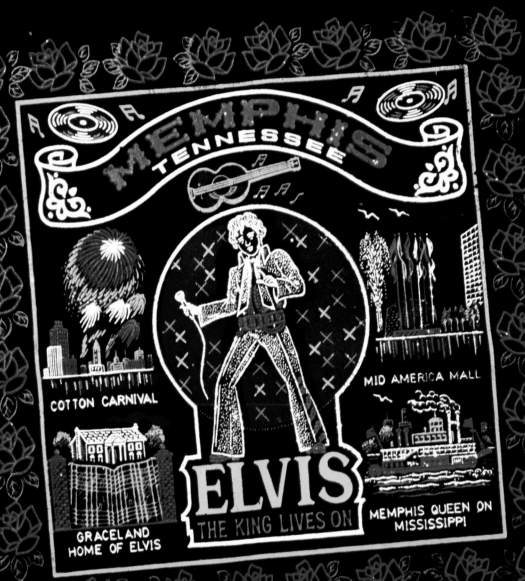

Taking Care of Elvis

Elaine Green is sitting in the Heartbreak Hotel restaurant on Elvis Presley Boulevard across the street from Graceland. She is smoking a cigarette and gazing at the pictures of Elvis that line the wall around the salad bar.

Elaine has come to Memphis from Tasmania with her daughter, Robyn. The plane trip lasted twenty-four hours. Their tickets cost six thousand dollars. To make the journey, Elaine (who is married to a truck driver) spent the better part of the last year selling Tupperware.

Because her T-shirt proclaims her a member of the Tasmanian Elvis Presley Fan Club—she is president of the 218-member group—Elaine has been barraged by inquiries about kangaroos and koala bears. She deflects the questions with the noblesse oblige of her office. She has not come halfway around the world to talk about life down under.

Today is August 14—the anniversary of Gladys Presley's death, two days before the anniversary of Elvis Presley's death. These are the highest holy days on the Elvis World calendar; and Elaine Green, like tens of thousands of others, has come to Memphis to pay homage to the man she has adored since 1956.

From Tasmania and Tucumcari they stream to the Mississippi River city that is home of the Beale Street blues, Holiday Inns, Piggly Wiggly Supermarkets, and Elvis Presley. All the motels near Graceland are fully occupied. Even the KOA campground outside town hoists the flag of Camp Elvis, its motor homes, tents, and trailers festooned with declarations of allegiance to the King.

The Days Inn, the HoJo's, and the Regal 8 on Brooks Road are transformed. Like college fraternities on pledge week, windows and balconies are draped with tapestries of Elvis. Doors to rooms are left ajar, inviting people in to trade or purchase rare records and commemorative decanters or just to hang out and talk Elvis with the family of fans—familiar faces that have grown old together over the last thirty years.

Strangers who enter will be asked, "Are you a fan?" The question does not mean "Do you like Elvis?" or "Do you think he was a good singer?" or "Wasn't he great in *Loving You?*" It cannot be answered with a casual "yes." To be a fan means that you have served hard time in the Elvis army. It means you have eaten macaroni and cheese instead of beefsteak in order to save money for an Elvis concert. It means you have camped in the rain outside a concert ticket office until your ankles swelled and your feet turned numb. It means you have driven all night and shared floor space in a motel room with ten other fans to be present at one of his performances.

When Elvis was alive, being a fan could be a party: having fun at the Graceland gates, hoping to catch a glimpse, jawing with gatekeeper Uncle Vester and the guards, who knew you by name; or "headbobbing" in Las Vegas. As described by superfan photographer Sean Shaver, "headbobbing" was a special nodding salute given by diehard followers to members of the Elvis entourage as a signal of solidarity. "The lobby of the Hilton Hotel in Las Vegas would look like a

ELVIS '86
THEY CAN
SCRAPE THESE WALLS
BUT THEY WILL
NEVER GET OUR
HEARTS... TCB
TOM SANOCK

YOU Entered My HeArt And
Touched My Soul, My Life
Will Never be the same!
I Love you !!!
Sweet Elvis!
Judy DeLuca
6-5-86

chicken ranch,'' Shaver recalls in *Elvis—Photographing the King*, ''with hundreds of people walking around nodding their heads at each other.''

Some fans will even tell you about the crazy good times they had searching through dumpsters in the backs of motels where he stayed, hoping to find the butt of one of Elvis's skinny cigars. ''We went through all the garbage cans,'' wrote Debbie Brown in *Elvis Now—Ours Forever* about the time she and some friends managed to get into a suite Elvis had just left at the Atlanta Hilton. They spotted burnt bacon, which they knew had been his. ''We grabbed it with gusto and guzzled it down.'' Then they tore back the covers of his bed in search of a pubic hair.

Now that Elvis is dead, that kind of wanton greed for a piece of him has been eclipsed by the need to cherish him. The fans have closed ranks, sheltering his memory from any two-bit journalist looking for a cheap laugh at his (or his people's) expense. The women of Elvis World tend to regard outsiders with suspicion, as protective of their hero as a pride of mother lions watching out for cubs. In their custody, Elvis's TCB (Taking Care of Business) coat of arms has been transformed into the motto of the posthumous Elvis Presley fan: TCE —Taking Care of Elvis.

And it isn't only fans who feel that way about him. Even a tough critic like Peter Guralnick writes in *Lost Highway:* ''It's all right, you want to say to him impertinently. It's all right. You did okay.''

Did okay? The man was a living god. He made millions of dollars. His dreams came true. But there is something vulnerable about the memory of Elvis that makes people want to protect and defend him. Fans are armed and ready with rebuttals for any negative comment, slur, or sleazy biography.

Their Elvis is a boy who loved his mother, who ''sir'd'' and ''ma'am'd'' everyone he met. He is Elvis the poor child who gave away his toys to those even poorer than he was, Elvis the man whose eyes misted over at the sight of the lame and the helpless.

''It is a good thing he had flaws,'' one fan told us. ''Otherwise, there would be a new religion in the world.'' In Elvis World, his memory *is* a religion. Like a holy rock-and-roller ghost, with mother Gladys at his side, Elvis sits on heaven's throne among the angels.

TAKING CARE OF ELVIS 167

Memphis in mid-August is almost always sweltering. Memphians like to stay indoors. But a week before the sixteenth, the streets in the Whitehaven part of town around Graceland start getting crowded. It is like a scene from Hitchcock's movie *The Birds:* first you see one fan with a camera and an Elvis button, then two in matching "Elvis Fan from Hoosierland" T-shirts, then four with bags full of souvenirs, then sixteen; and by the night before the death day, thousands are swarming everywhere around the mansion.

You can spot fans right away, because that's the way they want it. Many drive cars with vanity license plates announcing their passion: ELVIS, TCB, and EP are the popular formulations. With rare exception, the vehicles are big American sedans or vans, most of no particular distinction, except for the few Cadillacs and Continentals that evoke Elvis's own taste in transportation.

Women outnumber men; a majority are middle-aged, as Elvis would have been if he had lived. Nearly all have a T-shirt with an iron-on Elvis face, or at least a button with a sentimental motto such as "My Boy, My Boy."

These are not the Beautiful People. They are the hard core of Elvis World, and they know just how others regard them. Years ago, a fan named Shelby Townsend expressed it best: "We're the Elvis generation. Waxed fruit on our kitchen table, brand X in our cabinets, mortgage on our home, Maybelline on our eyes, and a love in our hearts that cannot be explained or rained out. He was one of us . . . the believers in magic and fairy tales."

On August 15, as the sun begins to cast its last rays across the portico of the mansion on the hill, the fans start gathering at the music gates. By 8:00 p.m., the street in front of Graceland is mobbed. In another hour, Elvis Presley Boulevard will be barricaded by police and all traffic diverted onto side streets. For now, cars drive past slowly, their passengers rubbernecking Elvis fans. Beer-drinking good ol' boys salute them with rebel yells from the cargo beds of passing pickup trucks. College kids cruise past calling out, "He's coming back!" and yodeling the spooky theme from "Twilight Zone."

A troublemaker in a passing car throws a coffee cup into the lap of a crippled fan waiting curbside in a wheelchair. And like the Seventh Cavalry in a John Ford western, along comes the Elvis Country Fan Club from Texas—two hundred strong, dressed alike in blue T-shirts and white pants or skirts. They form an enormous phalanx across Elvis Presley Boulevard as they head from the souvenir stores towards the Graceland Christian Church to the north of the music gates.

The Elvis Country Fan Club leads the candlelight service on the evening before the sixteenth. It begins with an informal singalong of "If I Can Dream," then "And I Love You So," followed by a recitation of the Lord's Prayer and a tape of Elvis singing "Lead Me, Guide Me," then "Suppose," and a final chorus of "Can't Help Falling in Love."

Although the ceremony isn't scheduled to begin until ten-thirty, by nine o'clock the crush at the gate is claustrophobic, elevating the evening heat back to where it was in the blaze of the afternoon. An Elvis impersonator wearing a leg-o'-mutton shirt scales the jagged stones of the wall near the gate and strikes poses to *Also sprach Zarathustra* played on a boom box. A large woman staggers and begins to swoon under the clattering weight of a floor-length vest with three hundred Elvis buttons attached.

Fans busy themselves inserting Elvis-faced votive candles into holders. We had been warned before we left home that candle holders are de rigueur for the service, lest one's hand get burned by dripping wax. Veteran candlelight marchers have brought hand-crocheted holders that they save just for this occasion.

At eleven o'clock, the music gates swing open with a motorized whoosh and the procession begins, guided by Graceland employees who have volunteered their time. "Please file silently and reverently up the drive to the meditation garden," the Elvis Country Fan Club instructs. And so it happens as the faithful make the long trek up the winding driveway to the garden where Elvis, Gladys, Vernon, and grandma Minnie Mae are buried side by side. On foot or in wheelchairs, dressed in overalls, muumuus, nostalgic poodle skirts from the 1950s, even an occasional tie and jacket, fans file up the Graceland driveway, past trees set aglow by the rainbow of red, green, and orange spotlights Elvis liked so much.

The path to the meditation garden is lined with floral tributes that have been coming to Memphis from around the world all week long, sent by individuals and fan clubs. Most are styled out of artificial flowers, hung with satin ribbons, further ornamented with teddy bears, wooden guitars, the TCB lightning bolt, and other icons of Elvis World.

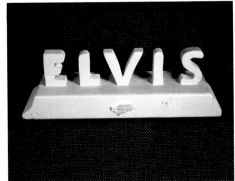

Elvis is a mesmerizing image for artists, whether rural primitives or urban avant-garde. Left: A back-booth shrine at the trendy Exterminator Chili Parlor in lower Manhattan. Upper right: Three paintings by Howard Finster, a Georgia folk artist whose Elvis iconography includes a childhood portrait and a paean to the Army days. Right: The apotheosis of Elvis, as shown in Mississippian Alice Moseley's painting "From a Shotgun House in Tupelo to a Mansion on the Hill."

Many tributes take the name of a song Elvis sang as their motif: "The Wonder of You," "Tryin' to Get to You," "It's Midnight." Others come in the form of souvenir offerings that give evidence of his worldwide dominion: "Love Letter from France," a hound dog from England, a tribute from Maine constructed out of pine cones around a large plastic lobster. "Just for the Record, We Love You" says a four-foot-diameter LP knit from black and pink wool.

More than a hundred and fifty of these tributes were made at Burke's Florist, just up the road from Graceland. Burke's is where Elvis bought his own flowers, so it is the preferred place for fans to shop. In honor of tribute week, Burke's has transformed its window into a *Blue Hawaii* motif, complete with floral guitars and leis and a mannequin (female) wearing a jet-black Elvis wig and painted-on sideburns.

As pilgrims approach the meditation garden, their pace slows. Their faces tighten into tragic masks. Some move their lips, delivering a silent message as they file

Some candlelight marchers feel heavenly joy as they wait to ascend Graceland's driveway.
Some shed tears as sad as in a painting by Keane.

past the grave. Single roses are strewn at the foot of the bronze inscription. Falling tears catch glints of the multi-colored lights.

This trek on the night of August 15 is deeply symbolic. It is a way to show respect for Elvis, but also a gesture for the world to see. Many of those who file past are the same people who loved him in 1956 when he was being condemned by the press, and in 1958 when the Army wanted to take him away, and throughout the movie years, and even in the final days when he began to falter. Now they are fighting the good fight again, showing to anyone who cares to look that they are faithful to the end, faithful beyond the end, for eternity.

Not all the goings-on during tribute week are sad or morbid. In fact, nearly everywhere other than at the candlelight service, the

For the anniversary of Elvis's death each August, fans from around the world send floral tributes for display in Graceland's meditation garden, where he is buried. The perpetual bouquets—most crafted from styrofoam, plastic flowers, wool, wood, and evocative Elvis World totems such as teddy bears and hound dogs—are one-of-a-kind mourning wreaths not to be found in any florist's catalogue.

mood is festive. At the motels on Brooks Road and the Howard Johnson's on EP Boulevard (where it is rumored Elvis used to retreat when life at Graceland got too hectic), Elvis Fests and swap meets make August in Memphis the happiest of times in Elvis World. Motel rooms are booked for the week and doors flung open to welcome fellow fans.

Original Sun discs, privately pressed tribute records, menus from Las Vegas shows, press kits from his movies, and paste-on sideburns are traded in conference rooms now reserved for memorabilia dealing. Nearly every bed and dresser and night table at the Days Inn is covered with ephemera for sale. Mint-condition copies of the 1956 fan mag called *Elvis: Hero or Heel?* are selling for one hundred dollars. Bootleg records are dealt from the trunks of cars parked outside.

Photographers offer complete sets of pictures from hundreds of concerts that they faithfully covered every time Elvis hit the road. Impersonators parade about in girder-sided "EP" eyeglasses, striking classic poses next to six-foot cardboard Elvises from movie-theater lobbies.

Authors autograph their books, one boasting that his custom-designed *Elvis Book*, in "living, loving color," is—at $155—"half the price of some liquor decanters." Ricky Stanley—son of Vernon Presley's second wife—sells a biography called *A Touch of Two Kings*. Ricky, whose long, ultra-blond hair gives him the fierce, theatrical look of a pro wrestler, grew up at Graceland, became a drug addict, then found Jesus and is now an evangelist.

Rosalind Cranor, doyenne of memorabilia (and author of *Elvis Collectibles*), has set up her booth at Howard Johnson's. She is selling original 1956 Elvis Presley Enterprises merchandise that collector Ted Young is dying to have. Ted took a bank loan to come to Memphis, and he has already bought an EP overnight case, the ultra-rare EP board game, and a drinking glass inlaid with images of the first five gold records. He has a Love Me Tender lipstick, but it has been used; he tells us he saw a mint-condition tube go for a thousand dollars to a Dutch fan.

Now Ted is ruminating over Rosalind's skirt. It is gray felt, original 1956-issue with a stitched-on outline of Elvis the Hillbilly Cat. It has a small, thirty-year-old pizza stain but is otherwise clean. Rosalind is asking five hundred dollars. Ted's jaw is working hard on a wad of chewing gum as he considers, hefting the skirt from its glass case and holding it up for close inspection.

T 16. 1977

ELVIS AARON PRESLEY

ELVIS PRESLEY BLVD

ELVIS PRESLEY BOONE HALEY
Rock 'n' Roll Battlers

PAT BOONE

PRESLEY full page ca

ROCK 'N ROLL STARS
25¢

THE REAL ELVIS PRESLEY STORY

BILL HALEY and his COMETS • CLYDE McPHATTER
PAT BOONE • FRANKIE LYMON and the TEENAGERS
LONNIE DONEGAN • THE PLATTERS • RUTH BROWN
FATS DOMINO • LA VERNE BAKER • LITTLE RICHARD
LITTLE WILLIE JOHNS • JOE TURNER • and others

ELVIS PRESLEY THROUGH THE YEARS
1957 mid-60's 1971 1977
King of Rock 'n' Roll
1935–1977

ELVIS PRESLEY – King of Rock 'n' Roll
1935   1977

#1
Large
Mini – $49.95

#2
Large – $125.00
Mini – $49.95

#3
Large $125.00
Mini – $49.95

ON STAGE
$59.95

ILOHA
$295.00

SILVER
Large – $300.00
Mini – $149.95

GOL
Large

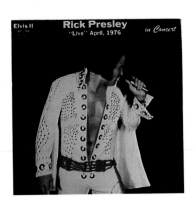

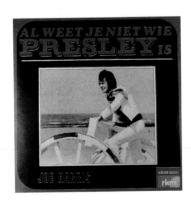

What the hey—he takes the plunge, purchases the skirt, and announces with an ecstatic grin that he is now flat broke. But his Elvis room back home in Oak Ridge, Tennessee, has been immeasurably enriched.

Fan clubs set up headquarters in rooms at the Days Inn. You can join the Having Fun with Elvis Club, the Something for Everybody Club, or the Burning Love Club. Love 4 Elvis focuses on "sharing memories, past and present, for the good times." Mile High on Elvis goes by the motto "God Blessed America, He Gave Us Elvis." Some are picture-of-the-month clubs; others trade records; most, including the club from Tasmania, do charitable things to keep alive his memory. Elaine Green explains that her club buys wheelchairs for those who cannot afford them—just as Elvis used to.

At the Days Inn motel, grass-roots capital of Elvis World during tribute week, people reserve courtyard rooms a full year in advance so they can compete in the annual window-decorating contest. Everybody starts with the same canvas: a door and a window with the air conditioner sticking out (very appropriate, considering how much Elvis loved air conditioning). The point is to turn this drab slab of motel wall into a vision of Presleyan beauty.

This year's contest is judged by Elvis's two cousins Billy and Danny Smith, along with seventy-three-year-old retired hairdresser Homer Gilleland. When asked by a reporter what his qualifications are to judge the window-decorating contest, Mr. Gilleland fishes among the chains on his neck to show off his bejeweled TCB pendant, then answers, "I did Elvis's eyelashes, hair, and eyebrows for twenty years." Mr. Gill, as he is known in Elvis World, is reported to have had a heart attack once while tending to Elvis's hair in Louisiana, although he maintains it was just some seafood that didn't agree with him.

First prize is awarded to mother-and-daughter team Alyce and Sheryl Peterson of Cincinnati for a display called "He Was Gone Then, Too, But Not Forgotten," a tribute to Elvis in the Army. They taped nearly three hundred pictures of his Army days on their window; they replicated his fatigues on a dummy; and they tied a duffel bag to the motel door. Both wear shirts with Elvis's Army medals, the insignia of his Spearhead Division (a lightning-bolt design that foreshadowed the TCB logo), even his Army ID number, known by rote to true fans: 53310761.

All of Memphis goes a little Elvis-mad during tribute week. At the Pink Palace Planetarium (former home of the man who started Piggly Wiggly supermarkets), one can see a laser show called "Elvis Legacy in Light," wherein astral hound dogs bop across the ceiling with the stars and planets. A night spot called Studebaker's sponsors a Priscilla lookalike competition, inviting contestants to mimic any of the Ages of Priscilla, from the Graceland era of the sixties to today's glamorous California look. (To the chagrin of bouffant lovers, audience applause elects a 1980s-style Priscilla the winner.) Libertyland amusement park offers a "Las Vegas–styled musical production starring Elvis stylist Andy Childs." Playhouse on the Square (in the Memphian Theater, which Elvis rented for private screenings) stages a one-act play entitled *Graceland*.

Serious fans stick close to Elvis turf and to each other. When they are not hobnobbing at the motels, they visit places that were his: Chenault's restaurant, where Elvis and his guys often repaired for biscuits and sorghum syrup; Humes High School, where young Elvis was once introduced at a talent show as "Elvis Teresa Brewer Presley" and sang "When I Waltz Again with You"; American Sound Studios, where he cut "From Elvis in Memphis," which many consider his greatest album; the Piccadilly Cafeteria, where Priscilla modeled clothes in fashion shows as customers ate catfish, cornbread, and ambrosia salads. Few pilgrims explore the city aimlessly like ordinary conventioneers. They tour the sights with a purpose: to be close to where he was, to breathe the same air.

At the Graceland executive offices (next to the Heartbreak Hotel and across the street from the mansion), there is a group of fans waiting to vent a grievance. Who knows how long they have been sitting, hats literally in hand. They do not read magazines, just sit silently watching the girl at the desk take phone calls. Someone comes out to speak to them. The problem: their copies of the *Graceland Express*, house organ of Elvis Presley Enterprises, was late in the mail. The delay is explained, and they leave, appeased, as unobtrusively as they waited. These are not the people who push their way to the front of the line at big-name restaurants; they do not have the arrogance of the rich and famous. They are remarkably polite. But of course they are: Elvis is beloved by them for his deference.

Each morning they come to Graceland Hall, a few doors down from the offices, to take part in an Elvis trivia contest, hosted by Graceland's communications manager and resident sex symbol, Todd Morgan. Todd is as cool as Pat Sajak of "Wheel of Fortune," but his wit

Sidney McKinney points to Elvis's graduation picture in his 1953 yearbook. In Elvis World, anyone who met Elvis is a celebrity. Mr. McKinney is especially important because he was one of the "short hairs" at Humes High School who chased Elvis through the halls, threatening to beat him up. Now a Memphis postman, Mr. McKinney will let you stand next to him in a photo free of charge. He has turned down $5,000 for his yearbook.

During tribute week, windows at the Days Inn motel near Graceland are transformed from empty glass to cut-and-paste memorial fantasies of Elvis.

is tempered by a low Arkansas drawl. He throws out stumpers such as "Who piloted Elvis's two-engine jet?" (Answer: Milo High.) The grand prize is a miniature of the Bill Rains bronze statue now in Elvis's racquetball court, called *Journey to Graceland*. But Todd is having such a definite effect on some of the ladies in the audience that they call out that *he* is the prize they want to take home with them.

Outside Graceland Hall, Sidney McKinney is walking back and forth amid the throngs with a copy of his Humes High School yearbook, *The Herald*, from 1953. He offers to pose with people or to let people pose with the book. With a thick index finger, he points out the graduation picture of himself, then, on the next page, the picture of Humes classmate Elvis Presley.

"I was one of the guys who chased him down the hall," he proudly explains, referring to that famous moment in Elvis World history when school bullies ganged up on him because of his long hair. "That's me," McKinney boasts, thumping his chest. "I was a crew cut and a fighter. I chased him all right."

"Didn't you like him?" we ask, confused because five seconds earlier he had showed us Elvis's inscription to him in the book.

"Oh, I liked him fine. I just didn't like his hair."

He points out the Class Prophecy on page 33: "We are reminded at this time to not to forget to invite you all out to the 'Silver Horse' on Onion Avenue to hear the singing hillbillies of the road. Elvis Presley, Albert Teague, Doris Wilburn, and Mary Ann Propst are doing a bit of picking and singing out that a-way." Mr. McKinney says he doesn't know what ever happened to Albert, Doris, or Mary Ann. Then we see the Last Will and Testament: "Donald Williams, Raymond McCraig, and Elvis Presley leave hoping there will be someone to take their places as 'teachers' pets'??????"

Why the question marks? we wonder, but Mr. McKinney doesn't know. In fact, he doesn't have a lot of time to talk, because so many people want to pose with him and his book. It is all done for free; he isn't asking any money for the privilege; in fact, he has turned down a collector's offer of five thousand dollars to buy the book. McKinney, who is a postman in Memphis, carries his *Herald* back and forth each year during tribute week because he enjoys the fame of owning it.

Sidney McKinney basks in a special aura reserved for those who knew Elvis personally. The further back the better. Having known Elvis—in any capacity—confers a glow that true believers relish. "Our curiosities about him," writes Hal Noland in his introduction to *The Life of Elvis Presley*, "will have to be satisfied through those who knew him and through the eyes of a photographer . . . for that's all that is left."

There seem to be few people in Memphis who don't have an Elvis story to tell. At Madison Cadillac ("The Cadillac of Cadillac Dealers"), Bill Spero recalls delivering a car to Graceland one night in 1968 and being whisked upstairs to Priscilla's bedroom by the staff—who, because of his genteel, silver-haired appearance, had mistaken him for the doctor. Priscilla had gone into labor and was waiting to be taken to the hospital to give birth to Lisa Marie.

The ladies at the open-all-night Gridiron Restaurant near Graceland regale customers with tales of wee-hours visits by Elvis and the guys in search of well-done hamburgers. Looking for one of his boyhood homes on Carroll Avenue (torn down), we found an ancient man who described Elvis delivering newspapers from the corner grocery store. And almost everybody remembers seeing their city's most famous citizen riding around town at high speed on his Harley-Davidson late at night

—the only time he could go out and not be mobbed.

"I knew him since before he was born," says Janelle McComb, who by virtue of her long-standing friendship with Elvis (from the time he was two) is now known as the First Lady of Tupelo. She wears a monumental diamond ring Elvis gave her and a TLC pendent ("Tender Loving Care," the distaff version of TCB), and she is a walking encyclopedia of Elvis lore. "I was there when he sang at the fair in Tupelo in 1945 [his first public appearance]," she tells us when we meet her in the parking lot on her way to address an Elvis seminar at Memphis State University, "and I was there at his last concert in 1977."

One of the most exalted artifacts in all of Elvis World is a poem Janelle McComb wrote at Elvis's request for Lisa Marie's fourth birthday. She called her work "The Priceless Gift," about the love between a parent and a child. Elvis autographed a copy for Mrs.

McComb; then, as he read it, he began to cry, and his tears fell upon his signature, blurring the ink. The poem stained with Elvis tears is now on display in the trophy room at Graceland.

One of the few people who can trump Janelle in closeness to Elvis is Lisa Marie Presley. But Lisa is a distant celebrity. On occasion she visits Graceland (which she will inherit when she turns twenty-five), but she—like her mother, Priscilla—is to Elvis World as a rarely seen Dalai Lama is to Lamaist subjects: too close to the gods to mingle.

Other relatives are not bound by any such interdiction. Uncle Vester, stepmother Dee, the Stanley stepbrothers, cousin Harold Loyd, and the Smith cousins are all prominent in the Who's Who registry. Almost all of them have written books telling what Elvis was really like. Dee, who married Elvis's father, Vernon, after Gladys died (much to Elvis's dismay), now manages an Elvis im-

personator. Vester, who used to stand guard at the music gates, still hangs out across the street at the souvenir stores, signing copies of his *Presley Family Cookbook*.

Whereas relatives can allow themselves to be passive and bask in the fame that blood or marriage conferred, former business associates and members of the Memphis Mafia work hard as Elvis evangelists to maintain their status in Elvis World.

When George Klein, president of the Humes High School class of 1953, longtime friend, and recipient of a new Cadillac, wrote a screenplay called *The King of Rock and Roll*, he said his goal was to be "in good taste and present Elvis in a positive manner." That is the idea if a former member of the inner circle is to maintain the respect of the fans: say something nice about Elvis.

All during Tribute Week, you can listen to the good guys get up on various platforms, or just wander from room to room at the Days Inn, reminiscing about the happy times. Charlie Hodge (a close member of the entourage who used to live at Graceland) and Eddie Fadal (disc jockey and Elvis's buddy during basic training), Joan Deary of RCA, Mr. Gill the hairdresser, and, of course, Janelle McComb, all delight in offering proof of Elvis's great sense of humor, his deep religious feelings, his love of the fans, his devotion to Lisa Marie, his charity, his humility, his generosity.

Do they protest too much? If so, it is because they are haunted by the theme of betrayal. Too many former associates have tried to cash in on their privilege or, worse, have become traitors. The heroes of Elvis World are engaged in an impassioned struggle to counteract the villains who would sully his name.

First among "the evildoers" are "the bodyguards" —Red West and his cousin Sonny, and Dave Hebler, whose book *Elvis: What Happened?*, published three weeks before his death, was a sensational account of drugs, temper tantrums, and megalomaniacal behavior. Stepbrother Rick Stanley calls it "the *major* factor in my brother's demise. . . . It broke his spirit. . . . It was what I call 'A Judas Act'!" It hurt especially bad because Red West had been with Elvis since high school.

Even worse on the list of SOBs in the Elvis World Who's Who are James Caughley and Lamar Fike, once two of Elvis's inner circle. They are widely known as the ones who fed Albert Goldman the dirt for his scandalous biography. And it is interesting: as much as fans revile Goldman, they seem to hate the apostates Fike and Caughley even more. Goldman represents the kind of pointy-headed snob that they have known to distrust

from the beginning, since the critics panned Elvis in 1956. You wouldn't expect an elitist academician like him to understand the appeal of a people's hero like Elvis. But Fike and Caughley—they're the modern equivalent of Bob Ford, the turncoat who shot Jesse James in the back for the reward money.

Just as there is a hierarchy of good and evil among celebrities in Elvis World, so ordinary fans take measure of their devotion. Those who have been Elfans since the beginning, those who actually bought an original-issue copy of "That's All Right," his very first record, are proud to feel that they have played a role in history.

Now that he is dead, they display their allegiance by keeping his memory alive—requesting his songs on the radio, placing an avalanche of phone calls to put Elvis way above Bruce Springsteen in a *USA Today* poll, joining the campaign to create an official Elvis Presley Day holiday, or demanding the issuance of an Elvis postage stamp. (They did it in St. Vincent in 1985.)

More important than being an early Elvis fan is staying loyal—through the movie years, through the weight-on late 1970s. "How many concerts did you attend?" That is a question to which all true fans have a ready answer. If you are like Len and Rosemary Leech of New Jersey, who were at hundreds of them, coast to coast, who devoted their lives to going to concerts and getting thousands of pictures, you have earned yourself a high position in Elvis World.

"I don't have any photos or snapshots of Elvis or personal experiences with Elvis," laments Linda Horr in her essay in *Elvis Now—Ours Forever*, "and saddest of all, I don't have any fond memories to share. . . . I'm so envious of anyone who has been to an Elvis concert. . . . I'll never know that kind of excitement and happiness. . . . I don't think any fan could love Elvis as much as I do, except maybe to the fans who have actually met him, the hurt is worse. If that is so, then I thank God for sparing me that kind of pain, for the loss I feel is bad enough."

Of all the many ways by which Elvis's memory is honored, impersonating him has got to be the funniest. Impersonators aren't supposed to be funny, but these caricaturists of human physiognomy are the court jesters of Elvis World. Nobody mistakes them for Elvis; but like sailors in the middle of the ocean who dress up in hula skirts and coconut-shell brassieres, they serve a purpose. They help you remember what the real thing was like.

Few impersonators (or imitators—the terms are used equally) try to look like Elvis of the 1950s. It is late Elvis who inspires them, 1970s Elvis, who was himself already an extreme version of Elvisness. Depending on the dimensions of the impersonator, the image ranges from slim "Aloha from Hawaii" Elvis of 1973 to heftier Elvis of the final years. The constant factors are thick peninsula sideburns and blow-dry black hair, wide belt, white suits (jumpsuits, if they can afford them—a good glittery one can cost two thousand dollars), and dark glasses with heavy silver frames.

Impersonators are all over America, all year round; but Tribute Week in Memphis is impersonator heaven. They perform at Bad Bob's Vapors Club on Brooks Road, they hang around the motels, they parade along the Graceland stone fence to the delight of crowds. Before you see one, you will likely smell him. He will be announced by a heavy cloud of Brut cologne (Elvis's favorite), as well as the aroma of whatever styling mousse he needs to get his hair to look right.

At the Days Inn, impersonators leave their doors open just like collectors and fan clubs, so people can stroll in and appreciate the Elvisness of their lifestyle. Their slippery rayon shirts and bell-bottoms are hung on motel hangers for all to admire; and their bathroom sinks are tonsorial vistas of hair dye, pancake makeup, mascara, hot combs, hair spray, and eyeglass-lens cleaner.

Who can pick a favorite among the Elvii? Some fans prefer the veteran pros like Johnny Harra, who performs in Las Vegas lounges and looks so right that he was featured in the semidocumentary film *This Is Elvis*. On the other hand, we have a soft spot for the free-lancers who hold down normal jobs yet manage to play the role anyway—guys like Oscar Wilde Martinez, a Hispanic Elvis from Waukegan, Illinois, who says he is "trying to break into it" and whose fiancée swears he

All around Graceland, Memphis overflows with Elvii—including Oscar Wilde Martinez (top), Artie E. Mentz (second from bottom), and Douglas Waxer (bottom).

sounds exactly like Elvis. Or Douglas Waxer, who drove straight down to Memphis from Detroit and whose motto is "Anything to Keep Elvis's Memory Alive."

What a magnificent obsession it is to look nothing like Elvis yet give it the old college try. To struggle to bend your New Jersey accent into the sorghum-slow drawl of a Mississippi boy, to disguise the fact that you are balding or wear four-inch lifts in your shoes and still get up only to five-eight. Some of them, no doubt about it, are pretty nutty—like the one outside Graceland's gates who insisted to us that his name was Elvis Presley. (If indeed it was, he would not be the first to have legally changed his name. At least one has undergone plastic surgery in service of the cause.)

Ronnie Allyn is so down-to-earth about being an impersonator that when he details how he does it, he might as well be selling you a vacuum cleaner and describing the attachments. Not that he takes impersonating lightly—far from it. It's just that he has a real down-home manner.

"First of all," he says as he eases himself into the plastic chair next to the air conditioner in his room at the Days Inn, "I want you to know that there are a lot of impersonators out there who are drunk with power. I know I'm not Elvis, but some of them forget who they are. I don't even like to be called an impersonator. I am an illusionist."

Nonetheless, it is a full-time job. He does not hang up his jumpsuit at the end of the day and forget about Elvis. In Pennsylvania, where he lives with his fiancée and vocal coach, Wendy Orris, the windows of his house are covered, Elvis style, with aluminum foil to keep out daylight. Like Elvis, he is a night owl. "My mother calls my house a mausoleum because of all the busts of Elvis and pictures of him that my fans send me. I have one bust that was done by an expert—even the eyelashes are painted on."

Ronnie is a master of minute detail. He asked Elvis's Hollywood hairdresser Larry Geller which hair dye Elvis used and followed suit, transforming his naturally brown hair into L'Oréal Excellence Blue Black, which he says is not at all easy to find. (He also uses Clairol.)

He is exceptionally proud of his hair, which he offers to let us run our fingers through. We sink up to the knuckles in its cologne-scented plushness. "Other impersonators tell me it takes them an hour to get it like this," he boasts. "I get up in the morning, run my fingers through my hair, and it's set. You should have seen me

Ronnie Allyn and his Elvismobile.

when I was ten. I had a super pompadour. My hair is just like Elvis's—real thick."

Ronnie learned his stage moves by studying karate. He trained with three vocal coaches for the singing, and a speech therapist to get the voice. He invested twelve thousand dollars in Elvis videos, which he studies; he spent two thousand dollars for his "Aloha from Hawaii" jumpsuit. He is as tall as Elvis, maybe even a shade taller. He is beefier, although if you put him side by side with Elvis of the mid-1970s, it would be a close match.

The substantial points of comparison between Ronnie and Elvis are matters of character. "I am an extremist. When I got into drag racing, I won a roomful of trophies. When I was in sales, I earned seventy-five to a hundred trophies from Alcoa. When I got into the Elvis thing, I had to have everything he had. I took it all the way. Ed Parker [Elvis's karate coach] told me that was just the way Elvis felt, too."

What Ronnie shares most of all with Elvis is his sense of humor. He is a card. He drives a white Lincoln Continental with ELVIS license plates and loves to listen to the truckers on the CB radio when he whizzes past on the interstate: "Hey, boy, Elvis Presley jes' passed me in a white Continental!" He has installed a tricky device under the hood so that if someone leans on the fender, the car speaks. "Please don't lean on me," says the talking Lincoln in its Elvis accent.

Ronnie's one regret is that his eyes are dark brown instead of blue. Otherwise, he is a happy man.

As boisterous as Elvis World is, Elvis's old friend Mary Ann reminded us how private and personal it can be, too. Mary is a one-woman conservatory with three things to show. We never would have known about her if we hadn't met her daughter in a YMCA near our house and if her daughter hadn't mentioned that Mary grew up with Elvis in Memphis. We called her, and she said she'd be happy to see us when we came to town.

The day we arrived in Memphis and telephoned, Mary was having a crisis. Her husband was at the doctor's office with chest pains. We offered to try and get in touch with her at some later time. No, she wanted to see us anyway; as long as her husband, Gerry, could drive, she would keep our date.

She didn't invite us to visit. She preferred meeting at our motel. She arrived with Gerry, who was okay but had been scheduled for an upper GI series and had to take a pill every thirty minutes. We all sat in our room at Howard Johnson's drinking water from plastic cups.

The Presleys had been Mary's neighbors at Lauderdale Courts. Mary wasn't a girlfriend, more like a sister to Elvis. When they met, she was sixteen; he was fifteen. The first time she saw him, he was sitting atop a twenty-foot billboard near the Courts, loudly singing "O sole mio." He shimmied down and introduced himself as Rudolph Valentino. "I'm Betty Grable," Mary answered, and they walked home together.

Mary brings out a copy of her high-school yearbook, *The Scrapper*, and brags that her school was superior to Elvis's Humes High because the football team was stronger. Her hands tremble when she opens the yearbook to the last page, where we see some familiar handwriting—Elvis's. "I hope some day you will be as pretty as I am (ha!). Just kidding. Love Ya—Elvis Valentino Presley."

Valentino? we ask. "That's what he called himself then," Mary says. "I remember when my girlfriend and I went to hear him sing at Overton Shell when he was just starting out [July 30, 1954], and I went to Elvis before the show and asked him to sign a photograph they were giving away." Mary now reaches into her manila envelope and brings out Exhibit 2: one of Elvis's earliest publicity pictures. She turns it over. The inscription reads, "Love ya, honey—Elvis Presley."

"I asked him," Mary says, her voice filling with portent, "What happened to Valentino?"

"Haven't you heard?" Elvis answered her without a smile. "Valentino is dead."

"And so he was now Elvis Presley," Mary concludes. The Sheik is dead. Long live the King. Mary breathes a shuddering sigh of relief at having told the tale, which has left her nervous and exhausted. We no longer wonder why she made the trip to our motel despite her husband's illness. Her Elvis memory is that important to her.

There is one final thing she has to show. From out of the envelope she pulls an old bent-edged snapshot she took when she was seventeen. It is a picture of four happy teenagers standing in a tight group on the lawn with Lauderdale Courts in the background. Three of them are goofing off with each other. The fourth, Elvis Presley, stands with his arms folded and a gaucho hat tipped rakishly back on his head. He is staring seductively into the lens.

We want this picture for our book! We stumble to the issue of buying the rights to use it. We suggest she set a price. She hesitates a moment, then says, "A million dollars." She isn't kidding. And we know if we offered her a million, she would jack the price up to two. Some things in Elvis World are not for sale.

Mary Ann slips the photo back into its envelope and clutches it to her chest. She is taking care of Elvis in her own private way.

Elvis World

Literature

Hundreds of books have been written about Elvis, in dozens of languages. We have chosen a variety (all in English) to provide the broadest possible perspective on Elvis World, from scholarly analyses to wacky cosmic séances with the King. Some are poetic, others are repugnant; each is, in its own way, an original. These are the books we believe belong in any serious library of Elvisiana.

HIS LIFE AND ART

Dundy, Elaine. *Elvis and Gladys.* Macmillan, 1985. It is unfortunate that the drawing on the cover makes Elvis look like comedian Jay Leno, because this is one good biography—about Elvis's relationship with the most important person in his life, his mother. The genealogy goes back to great-great-great-grandmother Morning White Dove, a Cherokee Indian; the account of Gladys's final days—and Elvis's helpless complicity in her decline—is wrenching.

Elvis at Graceland. Cypress Press, 1983. A handsome book with delicious pictures from the Elvis Presley Archives. While the text never ventures into anything controversial, it is readable and loaded with little-known details. Did you know Elvis had a pet turkey named Bow Tie? That he and Priscilla chose Noritake china (Buckingham pattern) when they were wed? That even though the mansion was centrally air conditioned, Elvis kept a window unit running full blast in his bedroom twenty-four hours a day?

Goldman, Albert. *Elvis.* McGraw-Hill, 1981. A gruesome, fetishistic biography that its author gleefully calls a story of "ever more bizarre sexual perversions, drug addictions and spiritual and mental delusions and hallucinations." It is impossible to overstate Goldman's meanness about Elvis the man, or his insensitivity to Elvis the artist. Collectors who are compelled to own one of everything—whether they like it or not—keep this book spine-in on their shelves so as not to spoil the view in their Elvis room. Fans blame the book not only on Goldman but on former Elvis employee Lamar Fike, who weighed nearly three hundred pounds before Elvis reportedly paid for stomach bypass surgery. Perhaps this was Fike's way of getting even for all the years his boss referred to him as "Lardass."

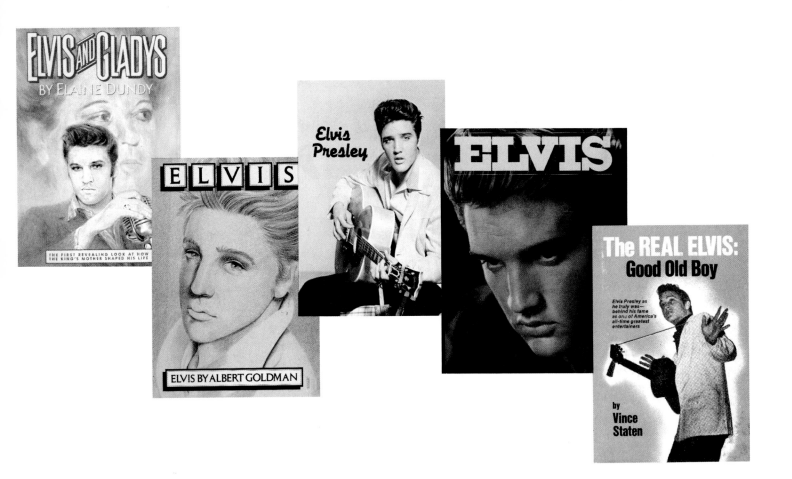

Guralnick, Peter. *Lost Highway*. David R. Godine, 1979. An anthology of articles about country and blues music, with two meaty essays about Elvis. Guralnick likes Elvis, especially rockabilly Elvis, and devotes his formidable intellect to the topic he calls "Elvis and the American Dream"—lauding him as a revolutionary force and lamenting that he was trapped by his success.

Hammontree, Patsy. *Elvis Presley, A Bio-Bibliography*. Greenwood Press, 1985. The author has taught courses in Elvisology at the University of Tennessee. Although her book is a rigorous, footnoted exposition of Elvis and Elvis literature, she cannot (and does not want to) disguise her reason for writing: she likes Elvis. Her interest stems from the 1972 documentary *Elvis: That's the Way It Is*. "I watched the film in disbelief as the camera panned an audience of upturned, beatific faces, oblivious to everything except Elvis on stage before them." She was reminded of "newsreel sequences depicting Mahatma Gandhi and his followers." She also thought of "audiences in Leni Riefenstahl's *Triumph of the Will*."

Harms, Valerie. *Tryin' to Get to You*. Atheneum, 1979. A friendly, large-type biography. The author founded one of the first Elvis Presley fan clubs, in West Texas in 1955. Her thought-provoking speculation: Elvis's classmates teased him in high school by calling him Gorgeous George. Gorgeous was wrestling's archvillain, known for his long hair and his odious vanity. Like Elvis, he was introduced to America courtesy of television.

Hopkins, Jerry. *Elvis: A Biography*. Simon and Schuster, 1971. *Elvis: The Final Years*. St. Martin's Press, 1980. The original Elvis biographer, Jerry Hopkins unearthed nearly all the data that now constitute the commonly accepted Elvis story. *The Final Years* tells a glum tale of decline in which Elvis eats too much, gets high, and tells one overweight employee, "You're so fat your toilet has whitecaps on the water."

Marcus, Greil. *Mystery Train*. Dutton, 1975. Taking its title from young Elvis's greatest song, this anthology of deep-dish criticism deals less with the man or his music than with the myth of lost innocence that Elvis seems to represent—especially to rock journalists. It is the defini-

tive "if only" account of Elvis: if only the Colonel hadn't enslaved him; if only RCA hadn't cheapened him; if only Hollywood hadn't beckoned.

Marsh, Dave. *Elvis*. Rolling Stone Press, 1982. A great big Elvis book. Although the pictures are edge-to-edge and copious, and in some cases rare, they tend to be oddly cropped, hard on the eyes, and underexplained. The text by Dave Marsh is what gives this book its oomph. Like many highbrows, he has a happier time with primitive Elvis, although his reassessment of the somnolent sixties recordings is a revelation. In the end, he concludes, Elvis "squandered it all."

Matthew-Walker, Robert. *Elvis Presley: A Study in Music*. Midas Books (Kent), 1979; Omnibus Press, 1983. Every recording session of Elvis's life is analyzed by a musicologist who skips the mumbo-jumbo about what it all means in favor of enthusiastic exegesis: " 'Heartbreak Hotel' is a basic blues, with a syncopated throb. The key, E minor, fits Presley's voice like a glove. . . . Floyd Cramer's piano is ideal: it is impossible to imag-

ine this song without his phrases high on the piano pattering like sad rain."

Nelson, Pete. *King! When Elvis Rocked the World*. Proteus, 1985. Elvis in the beginning, complete with reconstructed dialogue to flesh out the legendary moments. It even offers Elvis's thoughts: "Man, if they could only see me now, them goddamn freaks at High School who called ME a freak!" There are some fine, seldom-seen pictures of Elvis from 1954 to his Army induction and his mother's death. Then it stops: "The month of August 1958 was the beginning of the end of Elvis Presley."

Staten, Vince. *The Real Elvis: Good Old Boy*. Media Ventures, Inc., 1978. Author of *I Was a Teenage Teenager*, Mr. Staten first saw Elvis in 1955, after which he painted the hair on a ventriloquist's dummy black, named it Elvis, and won a fourth-grade talent contest. He focuses on the early years with a reporter's eye for detail: Elvis was so shook up when they didn't like him at the Grand Ole Opry that he left his costume in a gas station restroom outside of Nashville.

THE REAL ELVIS, BY THOSE WHO KNEW HIM

Cocke, Marian J. *I Called Him Babe: Elvis Presley's Nurse Remembers.* Memphis State University Press, 1979. A Presleyana classic, including snapshots of Nurse Cocke in the mink coat Elvis gave her, and of his bed at Baptist Memorial Hospital when he checked in with an enlarged colon. Mrs. Cocke made Elvis banana pudding and gave him the afghan she was knitting for Liz and Honeybunch, her two Chihuahuas.

Cogan, Arlene, with Charles Goodman. *Elvis, This One's for You.* Castle Books, 1985. Arlene is one of four teenage girls Elvis befriended at the music gates, then played with in the early days. These are good times: Elvis teaching the girls how to put on makeup, explaining why white panties are best, and eating a whole coconut cake by himself.

Jenkins, Mary, as told to Beth Pease. *Elvis the Way I Knew Him.* Riverpark, 1984. Mary Jenkins was Elvis's cook. A down-home tome with many pictures from the author's personal scrapbook, which make it irresistibly

charming. Mary recalls how she and Elvis used to listen to the "Gospel Jubilee" while he ate his breakfast; and she clucks like a mother hen over all the sausage biscuits he used to ask her to make. Includes recipes for vegetable soup, cornbread, and sweet macaroni salad.

Lacker, Marty, Patsy Lacker, and Leslie S. Smith. *Elvis: Portrait of a Friend.* Wimmer Brothers, 1979. Marty was foreman of the Memphis Mafia. He and his wife combine their firsthand knowledge with the literary skills of Leslie Smith, former correspondent for *Leatherneck* magazine. Like most of the insider books, this one contains great little moments of real life—like the time Priscilla accidentally chewed the legs off Lisa Marie's toy rubber spider.

Mann, May. *Elvis, Why Won't They Leave You Alone?* New American Library, 1982. Former Miss Utah, Hollywood gossip columnist, and self-proclaimed "very close friend," May Mann wrote her book at Elvis's behest: "May, publish my story," she says he told her. "I want

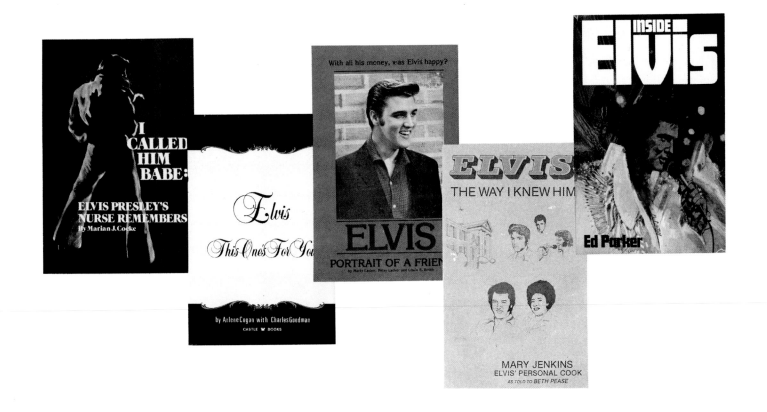

my beloved little daughter to know the truth.'' Chapters include ''Elvis Reveals All of His Illnesses, Including Cancer'' and ''The Buzzards Picking Elvis's Dead Flesh.'' Her tour de force is a ''You Are There'' recreation of the final moments: ''Elvis was seated on the toilet, actually reading a religious book . . . when suddenly a terrible pain gripped him in his stomach and seized his heart with a strangler's grip. 'Oh no, dear dear God,' he thought. He couldn't move. He couldn't get up. He had to get up. He must get up. . . . That terrible pain, like swords of fire, jabbing, slitting, cutting into his stomach, and especially his liver—it was impossible to bear. . . .'' As he lay helpless on the bathroom floor, ''suddenly the thought flashed through him: this must be like what Jesus suffered.''

Parker, Ed. *Inside Elvis*. Rampart House, 1978. Ed says he grew up on the back streets of Honolulu, where he earned the reputation as a fearless ''blalah''—Hawaiian for brawler. He says he is the father of American karate. He says Elvis referred to him as ''my second daddy'' during their seventeen-year friendship. Of special interest is Ed's telling of the time he and Elvis and Vernon watched a flying saucer from the backyard of Graceland.

Presley, Dee, and Ricky, David, and Billy Stanley, with Martin Torgoff. *Elvis, We Love You Tender*. Delacorte, 1979. Poor Dee. Ever since Elvis didn't attend her wedding to his father, Vernon, she has felt slighted. She used to call him ''my little Prince,'' in reply to which Elvis is alleged to have growled, ''I got your little Prince right here,'' grabbing his groin. Such stuff is *not* in this book, however, which—in Dee's parts—is devoted mostly to Dee's life as she ''glides in and out of the narrative in the same manner that she was taught as a little girl to enter and leave a room.'' Her sons' account of life with Elvis, on the other hand, is brutal—drugs, temper tantrums, etc.—even though they confess they had a lot of fun.

Presley, Priscilla, with Sandra Harmon. *Elvis and Me*. Putnam's, 1985. Ever the lady, the ultimate insider tells not all, but enough to keep the pages turning swiftly. Her sweetest story is the dinner party shortly after they were married. She baked lasagne for Elvis and the guys but forgot to boil the noodles first. Elvis crunched into his forkful, hesitated, then proceeded to eat his portion with gusto (and of course the guys followed suit), so as not to embarrass his new bride.

Presley, Vester, as told to Deda Bonura. *A Presley Speaks:* Wimmer Brothers, 1978. Uncle Vester, who manned the music gates for twenty years, was not only Elvis's dad's brother; he also married Elvis's mother's sister, Clettes. This book contains excellent early Elvis stories, such as the time Uncle Vester teased baby Elvis by threatening to steal his peanut butter and crackers. Afterwards, each time Vester visited, Elvis would yell to his mother, "Hide them, Uncle Vester is going to steal them!"

Rooks, Nancy, and Mae Gutter. *The Maid, the Man, and the Fans: Elvis Is the Man.* Vantage Press, 1984. Nancy was Elvis's housekeeper and continues to work at Graceland. She was one of the last people to see him alive. "On Elvis's last day, it was as though he had nothing wrong with him at all. I asked him that morning, 'Mr. Elvis, do you want any breakfast?' He said, 'No, Nancy, I just want to sleep.'"

Stanley, Rick, with Michael K. Haynes. *The Touch of Two Kings.* T2K, Inc., 1986. The kings are Jesus and Elvis. Rick became Elvis's stepbrother when the widowed Vernon married Ricky's mother, Dee. The reader is invited to "walk a mile in a three year old's sandals" and share in toddling Ricky's amazement when he and his two brothers woke up the first morning of their life at Graceland and "were greeted with three bicycles, three tricycles, three scooters, three little tanks, three machine guns"—courtesy of their new big brother, Elvis.

Stern, Jess. *Elvis: His Spiritual Journey.* Donning, 1982. The story of Elvis's relationship with Larry Geller, the self-described "hairnutritionalist" who enlightened him about Yogananda and Kahlil Gibran while snipping his hair in Hollywood. Includes: Elvis causing clouds to move in the sky, his ability to heal by the laying on of hands, and the revelation that he actually died of cancer—a fact the author says was kept secret "as it might appear to be a reflection on the singer's way of life."

West, Red, Sonny West, and Dave Hebler, as told to Steve Dunleavy. *Elvis: What Happened?* Ballantine, 1977. The book that outraged Elvis fans so much that some went on a campaign of gluing its pages together in bookstores. The former bodyguards said they wrote about his drug taking and erratic behavior to shock Elvis back to reality. They certainly did shock him. He died three weeks after it was published.

Yancey, Becky, with Cliff Linedecker. *My Life with Elvis.* St. Martin's Press, 1977. "The fond memories of a fan who became Elvis's private secretary." Becky cemented her friendship with Elvis when she threw up on him after riding the roller coaster at the Memphis fairgrounds in 1954. This is front-line biography from the Graceland office, but not the private living quarters. One learns, for instance, that when "Bunny" called, the secretaries were under orders to put her straight through to Elvis (Bunny was Ann-Margret's code name).

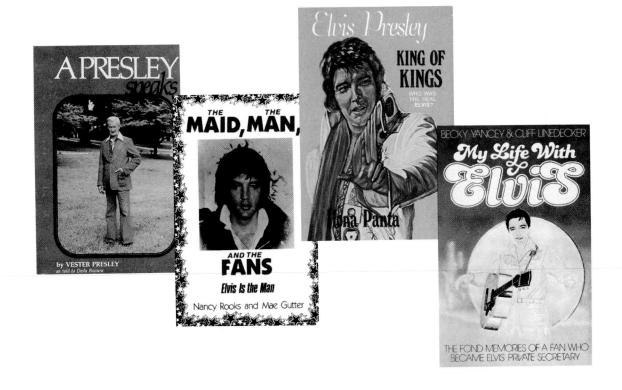

HAGIOGRAPHIES

Lichter, Paul. *The Boy Who Dared to Rock*. Dolphin, 1978. Elvis's life is rendered in many photos, but its meaning is buried under a mountain of trivia. The doting potpourri is upstaged by its author's own tumid biography: "Paul is a thin, dark, sad-eyed young man who looks and talks a bit like a rock and roll idol himself. His black leather hand-stitched trousers and embroidered multicolored shirt make a nice lead-in to the study in hair. There is his long black bob, his double-thick, heavy, black eyebrows, and the masses of coiled black hair on his exposed chest." Et cetera, *for four pages!* Elvis would have howled.

Lichter, Paul. *Elvis in Hollywood*. Simon and Schuster, 1975. Lichter reveals that he is a Libra with a collie named Elvis. Along with many stills and posters, the films are analyzed thus: "The film was funny and the soundtrack fair" *(Double Trouble)*, or "The story line was very simple and not very good" *(The Trouble with Girls)*, or "*G.I. Blues* showed us Elvis with light hair and a flattop. . . .The film was fun and the soundtrack one of the better ones."

Olmetti, Bob, and Sue McCasland, editors, *Elvis Now—Ours Forever:* Bob Olmetti and Sue McCasland, San Jose, California, 1984. The greatest of all fan books, made up of emotional essays contributed by those who loved Elvis, complete with snapshots, some so shaky or distant that Elvis is but a streak of light. Titles of the chapters are positively Zenlike in their distillation of the Elvis mystique: "A Dream Come True"; "My Elvis Blackout"; "The Red Velvet Hat"; "The Big Yellow Sunglasses"; "Elvis in the Snow"; "On the Bathroom Floor"; "How to Climb a Ladder in a Dress."

Panta, Ilona. *Elvis Presley: King of Kings (Who Was the Real Elvis?)*. Exposition Press, 1979. By means of astral surgery, the author and Elvis share the secrets of the cosmos. "The male voice continued to talk to me in a very mild and beautiful voice, and said . . . 'You just had brain surgery, and the two spirits are united.' In a joyful sound, he said, 'His spirit and your spirit are united, your spirit and Elvis's spirit are not two, but one.' " It is revealed that Elvis is the reincarnation of Istvan, son of Joseph, Archduke of Hungary.

Roy, Samuel. *Elvis, Prophet of Power*. Branden, 1985. The author idolizes Elvis, but his analysis of "the phenomenon of this century" is rigorous and compelling, organized semiologically in chapters such as "Money,"

"Residual Energy," and "Physical Appearance." Roy isn't afraid to say Elvis looked bad at the end, but he is never mean. Of special interest is his comparison of Elvis with Muhammad Ali.

Shaver, Sean. *Elvis—Photographing the King*. Timur, 1981. The best of many books put out by Elvis's self-appointed personal photographer. Shaver tells a breathless story of ten years dogging Elvis everywhere to get eighty thousand candid pictures. "I was shooting this concert with a new camera that looked exactly like a rifle. . . . Elvis saw it and screamed, 'Don't shoot!' then bent down as if making sure it wasn't a real gun."

Shaver, Sean. *Elvis's Portrait Portfolio*. Timur, 1983. Elvis the glittering jumpsuited legend as seen from the third row, rendered in a boxed edition, complete with text set entirely in script like a three-hundred-page wedding announcement. Bound in mock elephant hide, printed on paper so shiny you could use it for fingerpainting, the portfolio is less interesting for what it says about Elvis than for what it says about the man who devoted ten years to taking pictures of him.

Shaver, Sean, and Hal Noland. *The Life of Elvis Presley*. Timur, 1979. The text, by Mr. Noland, is based on memo-ries of Elvis intimates Charlie Hodge, Dick Grob, and Billy Smith. It contains oodles of detail for obsessives who can never get enough: When he appeared on the Frank Sinatra "Welcome Home, Elvis" TV special in 1960, Elvis had to be heavily made up to cover a scratched and skinned face he had gotten playing crack the whip at the Rainbow Roller Rink. While numbingly repetitious to a casual viewer, the hundreds of photographs (most of Elvis onstage in the 1970s) are a delight to idolators, who treasure every facet of the image, however subtle its differentiation from the others.

Shaver, Sean, Alfred Wertheimer, and Eddie Fadal. *Our Memories of Elvis*. Timur, 1984. Wertheimer and Shaver photographed Elvis at the beginning and end of his career. Fadal was his pal during basic training. Anecdotal text (again, in headache script), with a weird juxtaposition of photographic styles: Wertheimer's 1950s grainy, available-light journalism; Shaver's invasive assassin-with-a-camera sneak shots (supplemented by liberal dabs of white paint used to create highlights in Elvis's hair); plus a truly eerie photograph of what appears to be an outer-space baby that the authors assure us is "Elvis, only a few months old—by far the earliest published photo of Elvis."

Studying the Script

CATALOGUES

Banney, Howard. *Return to Sender*. Pierian Press, 1987. Howard Banney is the world's leading collector of Elvis tribute records. At last count, he had more than eight hundred singles and LPs, each featuring a song about Elvis, sung in the manner of Elvis, using a cut-in of Elvis's voice, parodying Elvis, or answering Elvis ("Yes, I'm Lonesome Tonight"). They come from thirty-three countries, from 1956 to 1987, recorded by artists ranging from Bruce Springsteen to Chito Berol ("The Elvis of the Philippines") to amateurs who have spent their life's savings on a white jumpsuit and an hour in the recording studio. Albums are detailed song by song, complete with a picture of their cover. The cumulative effect makes this book itself a staggering tribute to Elvis's continuing worldwide dominion.

Cotton, Lee. *All Shook Up: Elvis Day-by-Day, 1954–1977*. Pierian Press, 1985. Every day of Elvis's life about which anything is known is detailed: "1953. June 3 (Wed.) In the morning, Elvis applied for job placement at the Tennessee Employment Security Office at 122 Union Avenue. He was given the 'General Aptitude Test Battery' by Mrs. Weir Harris, and sent to M. B. Parker Machinists on the north edge of Memphis for an interview." Includes nine appendices: *Billboard* and *Variety* charts, all personal appearances, and a valiant attempt to untangle exactly what happened at the Sun Studio sessions in 1954.

Cotton, Lee, and Howard Dewitt. *Jailhouse Rock: The Bootleg Records of Elvis Presley, 1970–1983*. Pierian Press, 1983. An encyclopedia of the concerts, recording sessions, press conferences, and private-party sing-alongs that have been released on bootleg record labels. The listings range from albums that surpass the quality of anything RCA ever pressed to uncouth jokes such as *Elvis's Greatest Shit* on the Dog Vomit label.

Cranor, Rosalind. *Elvis Collectibles*. Overmountain Press, 1987. The definitive catalogue of what there is and what it's worth (old things only—no decanters or post-'77 ephemera), most of it photographed from Rosalind Cranor's own Louvre-level collection. Among the rarest of the items is a 1957 Elvis Presley doll, eighteen inches high with a "magic skin" body. Its scarcity is due to the fact that magic skin deteriorates unless it is rubbed regularly with baby powder. Rosalind explains exactly how to do it.

Sauers, Wendy. *Elvis Presley: A Complete Reference*. McFarland & Co., 1984. Biography, chronology, discography, filmography, etc., plus vital documents such as Elvis's birth certificate, last will and testament, and death certificate. Just the facts, ma'am: Did you know that on November 23, 1956, Louis Balint was fined $19.60 for hitting Elvis because he claimed his wife's love of Elvis was ruining his marriage?

Umphred, Neal, editor, *Elvis Presley Record Price Guide*. O' Sullivan Woodside, 1985. The complete catalogue of Elvis records, disc by disc, session by session, with detailed analysis of covers, labels, and different-colored vinyls. A monaural "Speedway" in mint condition is worth $600. "Tupperware's Hit Parade" (which includes "All Shook Up") is valued at a mere $60.

Worth, Fred L., and Steve D. Tamerius. *All About Elvis*. Bantam, 1981. Despite some egregious boners (*Jailhouse Rock* was *not* Elvis's first movie!), these 414 trivia-filled pages are heaps of fun. Listings include flotsam such as "Anzaldua, Nathan: Youngest professional Elvis impersonator (as of 1978) at the age of six," "12: Size of Elvis's combat boots," and "Tuesday: Day of the week on which both Vernon and Elvis Presley died."

DOCUMENTARIES

Burk, Bill E. *Elvis: A 30-Year Chronicle*. Osborne Enterprises, Inc., 1985. "It was my fate to be the lone reporter on duty (at the Memphis *Press-Scimitar*) during the night hours when Elvis would awaken . . . then begin cavorting around the streets of Memphis." Vernon Presley was quoted as saying, "Bill Burk wrote more good things about my boy than anyone." Here they all are; the only problem is that it is difficult to separate the thirty years of press clippings (which are fascinating) from Burk's interspersed reminiscences (also fascinating).

Cortez, Diego, with photographs by Rudolf Paulini. *Private Elvis*. Fey (Stuttgart), 1978. Paulini snapped his pictures one night when Private Elvis went on leave to a nightclub in Munich. They are strange, lascivious images of Elvis the innocent American being pecked at by Teutonic bimbos. The text seems to have suffered terribly in its translation from whatever language it started in: "Instead of coprophagic sublimations, Elvis-distributions of record-gift-capital-feces, we would have an oral politic not restricted to its anal version. Will the fecal Elvis promoted by capitalists reveal any internal contradictions?" As Elvis liked to say, "Right, chief!"

Farren, Mick, and Pearce Marchbank. *Elvis in His Own Words*. Quick Fox, 1977. Our choice for the worst-bound book about Elvis. The first time we cracked it open, all the pages cascaded out like autumn leaves. That exacerbated the major problem with this well-intended compilation of Elvis quotes, which is that none of what he says is annotated with where or when he said it. While the chapter titles are provocative indeed—"Elvis on Girls," "Elvis and the Critics," "Elvis Remembers His Childhood"—the words are meaningless out of context. Hideously grainy photographs: most appear to be copied from newspapers.

Gregory, Neal and Janice. *When Elvis Died*. Communications Press, 1980. A detailed account of the press reaction to Elvis's death, brightened with flashbacks to his life. The Gregorys reveal that the New York *Times* had no obituary prepared, that CBS misjudged the significance of the event by deciding not to run it as the lead story on the "Evening News" ("I may have been out of tune with the national consciousness," admitted producer Ron Bond), and that August 17, the day after Elvis's death, was the biggest day in the history of the Floral Telegraph Delivery Association.

Wertheimer, Alfred, and Gregory Martinelli. *Elvis '56*. Collier Books, 1979. Wertheimer was assigned by RCA to take pictures of Elvis in early 1956, on the brink of his cyclonic success. They are interesting (by now familiar) candids, but the text by Wertheimer and Martinelli creates images even more vivid than the camera shows. Here is how they describe Elvis getting off the train in Memphis after returning from "The Steve Allen Show" in New York: "At a stop in a rural suburb of Memphis that wasn't much more than a grass field turning yellow and a signpost that read 'White,' the Colonel let his boy go with a pat on the back and instructions to say hello to his Ma and to be good. Elvis swept his hair back and stepped off the train carrying only his records. We pulled out in the direction of downtown Memphis. Elvis, still dressed in his suit and white knit tie, drifted through the burrs and foxtails, wondering which way to go."

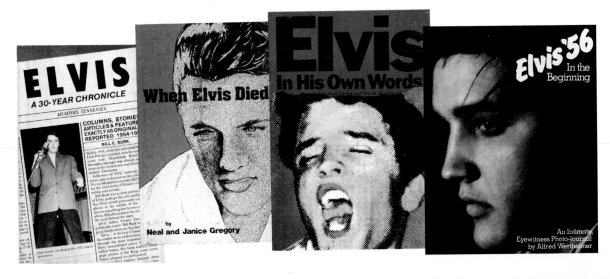

COOKBOOKS

Presley, Vester, and Nancy Rooks. *The Presley Family Cookbook*. Wimmer Brothers, 1980. This book reveals more about Elvis and his cultural milieu than many overwrought critiques. Recipes include Oatmeal Olive Meatloaf, 44 Karat Cake, and the classic Peanut Butter and Banana Sandwich. Highlights from Elvis's favorite beverage list are Gatorade, Bulghar buttermilk, and diet black cherry Shasta.

The Wonder of You Elvis Fans Cookbook, Volumes 1 and 2. R & M Crafts & Reproductions, 1985–86. Recipes contributed by fans and friends, from Don't Be Cruel Cauliflower to Change of Habit Butternut Squash. Proceeds go to the Elvis Presley Memorial Trauma Center in Memphis.

MISCELLANY

Cabaj, Janice M. Schrantz. *The Elvis Image*. Exposition Press, 1982. The tribulations of a Shaklee franchisee in search of Elvis lookalikes: The curtain rod at her motel breaks. Her frankfurter is served without mustard. The wax figure of Elvis she sees in Nashville looks like Glen Campbell. She does meet some good ones, including Jay Elvis via a contact at Skrudland photo, where she gets her snapshots developed.

Kelly, Joe. *All the King's Men*. Ariel Books, 1979. The world of Elvis impersonators in prose and pictures. Here are El-Ray-Vis, Little El, Big El, an optometrist Elvis who is managed by a Colonel, and girls who strap their bosoms down and put on jumpsuits. The photographs are reminiscent of Diane Arbus, but funny.

Panter, Gary. *Invasion of the Elvis Zombies*. Raw Books, 1984. Elvis as the inspiration for new-wave art drawn in the slavering manner of *Tales from the Crypt*. Captions read as follows: "The swamplike side-burned hip-slinging natureboy drags another crispy bicuspid girl through a quick boggy acre and into his smelly fortress of solitude." Includes 33⅓ record, "Precambrian Bath."

Pearlman, Jill. *Elvis for Beginners*. Unwin, 1986. A punk Elvis textbook from Great Britain. Art-schoolish render-ings of the life and meaning of "Our Butch Boy King" are interspersed with carloads of eccentric facts and wisecracks. "It's too bad Elvis wasn't cloned."

Tharpe, Jac L. *Elvis: Images and Fancies*. University of Mississippi Press (no date). Elvis for eggheads, written mostly by academicians. Essays on the man as socio-cultural enigma. Elvis as Billy Budd, Daisy Miller, and "The Memphis Faun." The most interesting (and least brain-straining) is by Nitaya Kanchanawan, a Bangkok professor who reports that "Elvis [via his movies] pre-sented one of the best pictures of the American peo-ple.... We always have an unpleasant picture of Americans who never care . . . [who] never listen to or respect their Elders. His love and devotion to his family touched the Thai heart.... We always said that 'He did just like a Thai.' Even when he divorced his wife, there were no hard words—'He still supports her, just like a Thai.'"

West, Joan Buchanan. *Elvis—His Life and Times in Poetry & Lines*. Exposition Press, 1979. A book of poetry dedicated "to the Living Memory of Elvis Aaron Presley, 1935–NEVER." Titles include "There Will Always Be an Elvis Presley," "Elvis and His Guitar," and "Elvis, We Miss You."

Acknowledgments

The cooperation of the Graceland Division of Elvis Presley Enterprises was invaluable in the making of this book. We thank Jack Soden, executive director, who allowed us access to photographic archives and always made us feel welcome at Graceland. Communications manager Todd Morgan contributed his vast knowledge about the life and art of Elvis Presley and never let us forget the magic that was Elvis. We also thank Patsy Andersen for never being too busy to help; and Joe Rascoff for giving us the green light.

It was Howard and Betty Banney who opened the door to Elvis World for us. We are deeply thankful for their enthusiasm, memories, and insights . . . as well as for guiding us through their magnificent storehouse of Presleyana.

Rosalind Cranor, queen of collectors, lent us her unique scrapbooks and helped us photograph her prize memorabilia.

Janelle McComb, lifelong friend of Elvis Presley, took time to answer questions no one else could.

Jimmy and Kathy Velvet took us into their wonderland of a home and generously provided many of the heretofore unseen images in this book.

Sarah Palmer infallibly rounded up hard-to-find newspaper and magazine clippings.

Patsy Hammontree took time to get us started in the right direction.

Photographers Bill Carrier, Jr., and his son Bill Carrier III searched their archives and delivered glorious pictures from Elvis's lost photo session in 1956.

Master photographer William Speer and his wife, Vacil, supplied their original large-format negatives of Elvis and his parents from 1955; the Speers came out of retirement to shoot us with the same artistry they had used with Elvis.

Maria Columbus dug deep into the files of The Elvis Special to supply rare pictures, as well as guidance, all along the way.

Charlton Publications—JoAnn Sardo in particular —magnanimously opened their Elvis files for us to use.

Bernard Lansky shared pictures from his personal collection, as well as his unique perspective as Clothier to the King.

Lew Eliot and Gust Smirnes ransacked their scrapbooks to give us the photos they took of Priscilla Presley in 1963.

For access to their photographic archives, we are grateful to Michael Ochs, Howard Mandelbaum, Carlos Clarens, Terry Wood, Don Lancaster, Robert Williams, Eugene Keese, Baer Frimmer, Pam Callicot, and the Blue Light Studio. We thank Hud Andrews for his lightning-fast photographic copy work.

Ted Young gave an eye-opening tour of his Elvis Room.

Interior designer William Eubanks shared his reminiscences of the redecoration of Graceland and took us out to a four-star feast at Justine's.

Tom Pittman of the Tupelo Journal provided key newspaper material about Tupelo's native son.

Patricia LaPointe of the Memphis Public Library

skillfully guided us through the library's photo and ephemera collection.

Mary Strnad gave us a firsthand account of life with teenage Elvis Presley in Lauderdale Courts.

Sue McCasland directed us to Sheila Flaherty, who lent us one of the greatest of all fan's-eye-view photos of Elvis.

Cary Jehl gave new meaning to southern hospitality by letting us use the incomparable Peabody Hotel as our home-away-from-home in Memphis.

Laura Crocker of Studebaker's nightclub provided a front-row view of the Priscilla Presley lookalike contest.

Lawhon School librarian Sara Parham took us on a VIP tour of Elvis's grade school.

Alice Moseley kindly gave permission to repro-duce her original painting, *From a Shotgun House in Tupelo to a Mansion on the Hill.*

For their gracious permission to reproduce the photos of William Eggleston, we thank Mr. Eggleston, Fred Acuff, and the Middendorf Gallery of Washington, D.C.

James and Judith Montieth and their children, Heather and Andrew, were always willing to babysit for Gus and Edwina whenever we went to Memphis.

We have saved the best thanks for last: to Bob Gottlieb, who believed in us—and in Elvis—from the beginning; to our editor Martha Kaplan, who has shared so much of our journey through Elvis World; to Iris Weinstein, who turned our jumble of Presleyana into art; to Mary Maguire, who knows the meaning of TCB; and to Bob Cornfield, the Atomic-Powered Agent.

Photo Credits

Celluloid Elvis

Gilded Elvis

Graceland

Looking at Elvis— A Portrait Portfolio

Wonders of Elvis World

Taking Care of Elvis

Elvis World Literature

All photos not otherwise credited are from the authors' private collection.

Elvis' Motorcycle

Vacation Fun

Steve Allen and Elvis

Soft and Mellow

Ready to Ride

Presley Press Conference

Strumming for Fun

Time Out
Between Shows

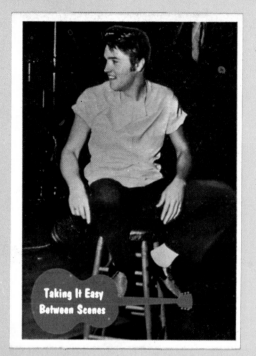

Taking It Easy
Between Scenes

Singing with
the Heart

Swinging Low

Elvis the
Actor

A Tux for TV

The Fan's
Friend

Burke's Florist,
Memphis.

A NOTE ON THE TYPE

The text of this book was set in a digitized version of Memphis, a
typeface designed in Germany by Ernie Rudolph Weiss (1875–1942)
in the mid-1930s for Mergenthaler Linotype. This was the earliest
modern revival of the French Egyptiennes types. In this design
there is a more thorough adoption of the slab serif, especially in the
lower case. An earlier series of faces named for the designer show
his fine calligraphic skills.

Composed by New England Typographic Service, Inc.,
Bloomfield, Connecticut
Printed and bound by Kingsport Press, Inc.,
Kingsport, Tennessee
Designed by Iris Weinstein
Jacket design by The Grimmett Corporation